Dear Dear Mary

Letters home from Amber

Edited by Jenny Melmoth

Illustrated by Jo Berriman

Copyright © Jenny Melmoth

Published by *Alfresco Books* in 2005.

Mill Race, Kirkby Malham, Skipton, BD23 4BN
Telephone: 01729 830868
E-mail: jen@alfrescobooks.co.uk

A CIP record for this book is available from the British Library.

ISBN: 1 873727 21 6

Cover design - Jo Berriman
Illustrations - Jo Berriman
Design and Typesetting - Jen Darling
Printing - Ashford Colour Press

Special thanks to ...
Jo Berriman for the beautiful illustrations,
Joan Poulson for editorial help,
Carole Baldwin, Angela Cooke, Mary Howarth (*Dear Mary*),
Jan Leavey, Graham and Harry Melmoth,
Valerie West and Gloria Wilson,
for their expertise and support.

1996

In April 1996 we lost our beautiful Daisy May. She was white with green eyes and a prima donna who knew her worth. It was a great sadness to see her soft coat turn dull and starey and know that she was ill. However, the vet was optimistic that he could find out the trouble and treat her. She was with him at the surgery for three days and nights, and then on the Friday when I rang, he said I could take her home next day as she seemed much better. But it was not to be. Saturday morning brought the call to say that Daisy had died in the night. It was cancer, a hard blow, bad enough to lose her, but worse that she had been away from home and I had not been with her at the end.

Trying to comfort me, my husband said, 'We'll get two kittens in a little while'. It was a tempting thought and would have taken us up to our optimum cat number again of four. There was a problem with our comfort plan however — spraying in the house. Silvester, who was our current, much adored, senior cat, had begun this rather noxious habit soon after the arrival of Bernard as a kitten. It had gone on for some years, but latterly had become less frequent. The vet agreed with us that, as cats are such territorial animals, the sudden introduction of two juniors could well precipitate a worsening of the situation again, just when the sprinkling of rose water was beginning to triumph over the less pleasant aromas we had endured.

While we were in this state of pause the phone rang. It was a good friend to tell me of a four-year-old cat in need of a good home. In fact, her owner was also in need of a good, if rather different, home. Mary, suffering with diabetes and failing eyesight, had decided (together with her family) that she was no longer safe in her lovely bungalow but should be living in sheltered accommodation. It was the last thing Mary felt she wanted to do. All her memories of her much loved husband were there; the garden was a pretty one and she had good neighbours.

Worst of all, Mary could not bear to part with Amber, and indeed flatly refused to be sensible and move to somewhere more suited to her physical needs until a happy new home had been found for her cat. It was not that people had not offered to take her, they had, but for Mary there was always a prohibitive snag — a busy road, young children who might tease her, a dog who might chase her, and so on.

Having confided her desperation to my friend, she, with her kind heart and knowing of our recent loss, wondered if Amber and I might help each other. Truth to tell it was a little too soon, especially as, in a mere four weeks or so, we were to travel to China and Malaysia, leaving the animals in the care of our son Hugo for ten days. Was there enough time to get Amber settled in before we left? Yet, given all the circumstances, how could we say 'No'?

This book is based on the original letters sent by Amber to her Dear Mary following their enforced separation. Since, inevitably, they can only reflect events from a cat's perspective, some dates and linking passages have been added to help clarify the wider picture.

6th May

Dear Dear Mary,

What is going on? I rather liked that Jenny person who came to see us the other day, even though I had to come in from the garden specially to talk to her. As you know I'm quite particular about making friends, but I thought she was all right — she had a comfy lap. But I was surprised that you allowed her to upset you today by putting me in a basket and taking me away from you. I don't enjoy rides in those noisy tin cans and this was lengthy travelling and made me trembly. I'm not delighted about being in this new place, though it seems fairly comfortable.

There's a very large bed, which is good for hiding under whenever I feel frightened, which is quite often, as the place is full of strange sounds and smells. The new person keeps coming in and talking to me. She brings me milk and food, and seems harmless enough. Sometimes she stays awhile on the bed and talks into a funny white thing with buttons and a long silvery whisker. I suppose I will be all right for tonight at least, but it helps to think about you. Do you remember how frightened I was before I came to live with you? I'll do some remembering for you tomorrow.

Purrs of love,

from Amber

6

Dear Dear Mary,

More people have been to see me. The Jenny Person brought her mother this morning and she was very gentle and quiet, a bit like you Dear Mary.

Do you remember the first time I saw you? I was only a big kitten, a few months old. I'd been having a horrible time. After I was taken from my own warming mother nothing was nice. I had two brothers and they were taken away by some small people and their parents, but no-one seemed to want me. I was growing bigger and my mother had been saying it was time I left her and had a home of my own. Then one day the shouting man who lived in the same house as my mother (she didn't like him) stuffed me roughly into a smelly bag and carried me for hours and hours before pulling me out and saying, 'Time to look after yourself pussy-cat. Go and catch mice, that's what cats are meant to do isn't it?'

He then left me in a dark hedge and it was cold. The world was so big. I felt smaller then than the day I was born. I was so very frightened. I sat more still than still for days and nights. But then I got so hungry I moved slowly, slowly, towards a huge building where there were tempting smells of food.

Speaking of which, the Jenny Person has just come in with my tea. She's not a bad person at all, but I think she must be lonely, for she sleeps on the bed with me at night and I purr to her when I feel like it. I know she's been talking to you, using that white lump with the buttons and long silvery whisker. I think it must be what you used to call 'the phone', though it doesn't look the same. She's been telling you how I am and you've been saying you're so sad without me. Why am I here then and when am I coming home Dear Mary?

Loving purrs,

from Amber

Dear Dear Mary,

I had a fairly comfortable night keeping the Jenny Person company again. There's a man living in this house as well, but not like your Dear Albert who was always there with us. This one is only about in the evenings and in the early morning. He's visited me once or twice and has a deep, but not rough, voice. The Jenny Person seems to like him, but she'd rather stay with me at night. However, she goes to talk to him in the mornings when we wake up. I was awake first today and sat on the sill looking out of the window. A big black-and-white chap went by in the garden. Of course, I was so high up he didn't see me but I think he lives here too. I'm sure I've smelt him under the door.

The Jenny Person has just brought me my breakfast but I don't feel hungry. I'm missing home, missing you, missing outside. Oh, Dear Mary, the garden looks so good, what wouldn't I give to get out there, climb some of those trees and scrabble in some proper earth instead of in that silly grit in a box. I can't bring myself to use it until I must.

Anyway, where was I with my remembering yesterday? ...

Yes, I was in a cold, cold hedge with tempting smells coming from a huge big building nearby, and I quietly crept and crept, closer and closer to the lovely smells. But then I saw feet, big feet, and there was a long horrible stick with a flopsy wet head on it that attacked me with a wild squashing shout. I yowled and ran faster than a mouse back to the hedge.

Then later, Dear Mary, some of those small people you call children chased after me, and were trying to poke me and get me out. It was the most horrible thing that had ever happened to me, and I thought, well I'm not very big and I'm not very old and I'm never going to grow any bigger or older. I was trembly and spitty all over. I just went deeper and deeper into the bushes and decided never ever to bother to eat or drink or do anything ever again. It was my ending. Only it wasn't.

All day long I got more and more miserable, and hungrier and hungrier. Every time I heard voices and the children running about, I felt trembly and kept still, not moving a whisker, and they soon forgot about me.

At last it went silent and then began to go dark. But before it became night I heard a different sort of noise, very quiet footsteps and then a voice talking properly. Even though I didn't understand all the words I knew this person would not hurt me and was saying something like, 'It's all right little cat you can come out and talk to me, for I'll keep you safe and look after you'. And I liked the way the voice kept singing, 'Here kitty kitty kitty, here kitty kitty kitty', until at last I began to think that maybe I would just creep a bit closer to see what I thought. So I did, though I was still very, very frightened. But I saw a big smiley face and a person kneeling down with a dish of food, and it smelt so good, so very good, that I crept nearer, ever nearer, and the voice was singing and singing that it was all right. So I started to eat, and then to gobble, and I forgot for a moment the big smiley face as the food was *so* good. Then suddenly a big hand gripped me on the back of my neck, just before I'd even thought of rushing safely back into the bushes, and I was plonked in a basket and the lid was shut. Well really, I know she meant well, but fancy interrupting my meal when I was so hungry, and still so frightened too, though not quite as much as before as the voice went on singing.

Oh, Dear Mary, the Jenny Person has just interrupted my remembering. She's carried me into a big new room with another bed in it and a dog lying on the carpet. Dog is rather large but very quiet and the same colour as me. I feel safe here. Jenny puts me on the bed and I look down at Dog who takes **no** notice of me at all. I'm not sure if I should be insulted about this. I mean, she just doesn't even seem to know I'm here, so I think I'll tell her. I leap air-lightly onto the carpet and slowly, slowly creep up to her and sniff her tail, then her back feet. And Jenny says something like, 'Good girl Rosie' and 'You see it's all right Amber', and Dog lifts her head a tiny bit and just looks at me as if I'm boring, then goes back to sleep. Well, I feel a bit offended, but not at all frightened. And Jenny picks me up, cuddles me and tells me I'm beautiful, which is true. Then she holds me up so I can see more of the garden that seems to belong with this house.

... And I can't manage any more today Dear Mary.

With purrs of love,

from Amber

Dear Dear Mary,

I'm feeling upset so am under the bed thinking about you. Dog came into my room a little while ago, but she just walked round quietly, then left, so that was all right. But then Jenny brought that big black-and-white chap in to see me. I was on the bed and she was holding him up on high, which would have been fine except that he growled at me which I thought was rather insensitive. I mean, I didn't ask to come here did I?

So I've come under the bed where I feel safe. I hope you're safe too, Dear Mary, without me to look after you and keep your knees warm in the evenings. I remember the first time I saw you, your voice was so gentle. I was in a big room in a cage thing where there were other cats and the Singing Person sang to us all. I didn't much mind being in a cage. I felt safe there and it was so much better than being in the cold, dark, windy outside with no food. I'm not sure how many hours I was there but I ate a lot before you came.

Then the Singing Person took me out of the cage and put me on a table, where I walked up and down, showing you my beautiful tail and how I could be happy if only I had the chance. The other cats in the cages were watching me and saying that they'd like to go home with you too, but you said,'Oh no, she's lovely, she's the one, I wanted a ginger cat. Will you come home with me and I'll call you Amber?' I pushed against your hand and it was warm like my mother. Then you picked me up and cuddled me close and I felt warmer still and knew I'd found a home of my own at last.

However, I was not so keen on the journey in that moving room. Why do people insist on going everywhere in one of those things? The Singing Rescue Person had one, you had one, and now Jenny has one. You're all very restless. Me, I like to be in one place, with my own door so that I can go out, come in, then go out again. So cages of any kind are not usually a good idea. Choosing my plan for the day (and night) takes time and concentration too. I remember it took me a little while to teach you that Dear Mary. We had a few muddles didn't we?

I'm a fastidious cat, exceedingly fussy about my toilet arrangements. I like them to be personal, private and sparkly clean, which was why, when I first came to your house I thought the bath was ideal, with that thoughtful hole provided at one end. Of course, I was still only young then and didn't even know how to work the cat flap to outdoors. You told me very gently that this was not the usual way to use a bath and took me outside to the soft scrabbly earth. Personally I still think it wincing odd that people enjoy drowning themselves in baths of hot water so often.

Bemused purring,

love Amber

PS   Jenny has just taken me with her into a big white room with a bath, and a basin in which she buried her head in the water. Ugh! People do such strange things. Fortunately I don't have to go near the water but can sit on the wide, friendly window-sill and watch the trees outside. I wonder if she knows I'm good at being outside?

PPS I had liver again for my nightcap — just like at home.

Dear Dear Mary,

When I woke up this morning I felt a bit bored, so I pounced on Jenny's toes under the covers. She seemed to like this. It made her laugh. I was glad. I like making people happy.

Oh Dear Mary, there's a lot of house to get used to. Today Jenny carried me down to the kitchen and I sat on the window seat. Then this huge powerful lion bashed up onto the table. I didn't like him **at all** so I growled, but he didn't do anything, just sat there and looked at me, which made me nervous. So I got down to go back to my camp under the bed — if only I could have remembered where it was. But then he chased me and I had to hide under anything I could find, which was a big sofa in a room I didn't know. I hid and spat, and the lion would have pounced on me, only Jenny picked him up and took him away, which was brave of her I thought, though she seems to like him. It's no use trying to understand the way people think. Oh Dear Mary, do you think the lion cat lives here all the time? I do hope not. Never mind, perhaps I can come home to you soon. I'm getting twitchy whiskers about not going in the garden. I wonder if she'll ever learn that's what I'm used to.

Do you remember how I used to like helping your Dear Albert in the garden? I loved to sit on the wall in the sunshine while he worked and worked making the flowers grow. Sometimes I'd climb into his wheely-barrow to get a closer view, and one day he pushed me round the garden in it. I didn't mind, especially as it seemed to please him. Then, when the small young persons came, they would ask to take me for a ride and they pushed the wheely-barrow quite fast, and laughed and laughed, and so did you and Dear Albert. And they said I rode like a queen in a chariot, and it made me happy to make so many other people happy. But I was younger then and brave, and you were there.

We had so many lovely times. What about when I found Dear Albert digging a big hole, and you were crying and he was too, and I just walked up and said, 'What's the matter, can I help?' You looked at each other and cried some more, but laughed as well, then picked me up, and cuddled and cuddled me. I must say, Dear Mary, that I thought it was very strange. I'd only been in the bushes sleeping awhile in one of my camps, but you kept saying, 'Oh Amber, we thought you were dead. Oh Amber. Oh

Amber.' And I thought, well yes I know who I am. And then suddenly I saw and understood. There was this poor ginger cat, all stiff and smashed up, and Dear Albert was putting it gently into the ground. And I was glad it wasn't me, but sorry for the cat that was dead. Then I thought again how roaringly-dangerous was the horrible road near our house, where I would never go.

I've just noticed ... Jenny has left the door to my room open. Perhaps in a little while I will be brave and have a look round.

With loving purrs,

from Amber

Lion — fiercely big and mighty!

Dear Dear Mary,

What do you think? I'm Amber the explorer. Jenny went out for a long time and Dog went too. As I said yesterday, the door to my room was open so I crept very carefully out onto the place with the stairs and then into the room where the man sleeps. Fortunately, there was no sign of the big black-and-white chap, nor of the fierce lion cat. I seemed to have the upstairs of the house all to myself. What I liked best was the window-sill in Jenny's room, where she's got lots of books and writing things, and a good view of the birds on the roof. Then, in another room, there's a beautiful white bath which is fun to walk in — when it's empty of course. I wouldn't go near when it's full of hot water and drowns people.

Oh, and I've been outside Dear Mary, only that was later when Jenny came home and took me. First I went in her arms and she walked round all the trees and I thought it looked good, but I wasn't too impressed when she fixed a red, long, stringy thing to my new collar. (I may have forgotten to tell you that one of the strangest things that Jenny has done so far is to put this collar on me with a clinkly-tinkly thing hanging from it, which she says is to stop me getting lost. I can't think how, can you?) To feel my feet on the fresh grass made me purr in a special way, but I was attached to Jenny somehow so I couldn't move freely, which was rather undignified and spoilt the softness of the earth under my paws. For a kindly person she's really rather stupid, Dear Mary. Surely she should know that I want to get to know the garden in my own way.

Do you remember how I loved to play with the gentle water from the hose when Dear Albert was giving a drink to his plants? I think it was a big help to have me there to tickle the water and make him smile. And the plants enjoyed it too because they grew and grew.

I've had a busy day today and am glad now to be back in my own room thinking about you and your comfy lap — the comfiest lap in the whole world. No-one could ever have a comfier lap than yours Dear Mary — warmly, deeply, widely, softly comfy.

Lap-kneading purrs,

love Amber

Dear Dear Mary,

Maybe because I was thinking about your lap, and because I went out in the garden for the first time yesterday, I had a dream in the night ...

The Singing Person was with me in a garden somewhere I did not know and she was stroking me and saying, 'Your Dear Mary loves you best Amber'. And as I rolled on the grass in the sun, Dear Albert walked up with his wheely-barrow and said, 'Hello Amber, I must do some tidying up.' Then he took his saxyphone out of the wheely-barrow and played a silvery tune as we walked softly through some trees together, until he was suddenly gone and it was night-time, with a robin sitting against the moon singing, 'This way, this way ...'. So I followed my whiskers onto the seat of a tin can that moved without a sound along a winding way, till you opened the door, Dear Mary, and lifted me out saying, 'Oh Amber, I *am* glad you're home for I need you to eat up all this liver.' And there on the kitchen table was a huge meaty heap, purring happily to itself. I thought, 'I hope it will wait for me to jump up.'

Then I woke up and was on the bed in my room feeling even more than usual that I should not be here, but safe at home with you. And I wished for my dream back again, but it would not come and I am sad.

All my loving purrs,

from Amber

Dear Dear Mary,

I miss you, especially after my dream. I've been thinking about all my old favourite places, like my wall in the garden, where I used to watch and help Dear Albert and your friendly friend next door in her garden. I was sorry afterwards that I caught her robin; I didn't mean to upset her. It's not purry being upset is it? And I should know. I thought I was all right here, but this morning when my door was open again, Lion came in and looked at me. Fortunately, I was in my cave under the bed, and all he did was look and look with his fierce eyes. I tried to stare back at him but I didn't like it, it made me feel trembly.

So I'm having a quiet day today resting in one of my boxes. Jenny keeps two or three under my bed with interesting bumps in them which she says are for 'presents' though why anyone would want to be given bumps I don't know. But the towels on the top are quite comfortable and not even Lion dares to come into this under-bed territory. I've felt like a not-coming-out-much-day today, though early this morning I went into Jenny's bedroom. However, I've been thinking and thinking, and am beginning to have an exciting idea about the dream and what it could be telling me.

Purring hopefully,

love Amber

Dear Dear Mary,

Soon I will tell you what I've been thinking, which is helping me to be more cheerful, and I've had a good day exploring upstairs again. It's sunny in Jenny's bedroom and I lay on the carpet and watched the garden through the big glass window-doors, which were open a little so I could feel the fresh air. And outside I saw some huge black-and-white animals. Oh, Dear Mary, they were so surprisingly big I couldn't take my eyes off them. I mean, the black-and-white chap here is big enough for me, but they made him look silly, which is the name Jenny calls him sometimes. 'Hello Silly Cat' she says. There's a lot here I don't understand. I don't like him much but he's a lot better than Lion and seems quite sensible.

Anyway, the enormous black-and-white animals didn't do a lot, just munched grass loudly. I only eat grass if I feel a bit ill, so perhaps they'll do other things when they feel better. Jenny took me outside this afternoon so I saw them close-up. They didn't frighten me much but I just wished that I hadn't been on that lengthy string again. I know I've only been training her for a few days, but Jenny should have realised by now that I don't like it. However, I suppose I'll just have to be patient and realise that not everyone can be as quick to understand me as you were Dear Mary, and that she may not have time on her side.

Wistful purrings,

love Amber

Silvester — Jenny's 'Silly Cat'!

Dear Dear Mary,

Rather a boring day today, but restful, like one of our cold rainy days at home, when we would both stay in and I'd sit on your lap for a long time, as long as you didn't get up to do things. Jenny went out quite early today, soon after I'd eaten my breakfast, with which there were some funny round biscuits and not so much meat. I think I quite liked them, but they were different from anything I've ever had before.

Fortunately, Jenny's mother came to visit, whom I first met very soon after I arrived. I purred for her quite a lot and she stroked me gently. We like each other and I let her take me into the room that Jenny shares with Man, where we sat and looked at the huge black-and-white animals. 'Cows they're called', she said. We watched them for a long time but they still didn't do much. Then Lion fell out of a cupboard with a great thump and stormed through the room, which was enough to frighten me, though he didn't do anything except glare like fire, then disappear through the door. The Gentle Mother cuddled me to make me feel better and then I was ready to go back into my own room.

Later on I noticed Lion was peering at me through the window. I'm sure I could climb that tree just as well as he can if only I had the chance. Anyway, what did it mean? Does he like me or hate me? I hope he likes me, because he's fiercely big and mighty, though it may not matter greatly, for the idea I have is growing and growing all the time.

I'm thinking, Dear Mary, that my dream was telling me to go bravely, trusting to my whiskers and following them like I did in the dream. If I do, then I may be able to find my way home to you. Of course I must wait for Jenny to set me free from the silly string and, meanwhile, I'm eating all I can to make me strong for travelling.

Jenny was purring pleased to see me when she came home later in the day. I expect she would be sad if she knew about my dream of coming back to you, to my own proper home, don't you?

Planning purrs,

love Amber

Dear Dear Mary,

Quite a lot has happened besides planning my idea. Yesterday Jenny took me to see the vet man. I was not pleased. It meant going in her room-on-wheels again, inside that horrible basket with a lid, which is fur-rufflingly undignified. Then the vet's house has such a strange smell and feel to it. Frightened dogs are huffing and puffing, cats are mewing, and people are having silly conversations about us all as if we don't understand what they're saying. I think it's very hoity-toity of them, don't you Dear Mary?

You hadn't taken me to the vet for a long time because you know I don't like it, but Jenny maybe didn't know that. Well who would like it? I mean the vet man stuck a needle in me, looked in my mouth and said I had 'ginger-ightis' and must have some toothpaste. He's a kindly man, and probably a good vet, but I did wonder about his sense. What can my ginger colour have to do with my mouth's inside? Do black-and-white cats need toothpaste too?

Talking of my colour, do you remember, Dear Mary, saying to me one day, 'Oh Amber you are so beautiful now. When you first came your coat was pale like primroses, but now it's as deep and golden as lilies'. And we looked at those tall flowers that Dear Albert had grown, and you smelt them and said, 'And do you know Amber your fur smells as sweet as flowers'. Then I felt very purry indeed, and we both smiled.

Oh, the vet also said that liver isn't good for me and Jenny said she knew that but I was used to it. (I most certainly am.) She then told him that when I was more settled she wouldn't give me any more. Oh, Dear Mary, I'm not sure I like the sound of that. Anyway, she brought me some tonight, though not quite as much as before, but a biscuit or two helped, and she does give me a lovely cuddle at night and whenever I feel like it. She does try so hard and, considering she's not you, she doesn't do too badly, but I hope she won't take me to the vet again.

If I can make my dream come true then she won't have the chance will she? But I'm still on that silly string in the garden.

Patiently purring,

love Amber

Dear Dear Mary,

Well, I can't say I like the toothpaste that Jenny's rubbing round my teeth though I think my mouth feels soothed. I was remembering how the first vet man I ever saw, who had something to do with the Singing Person, made me go to sleep and when I woke up my side hurt and some of my beautiful primrose fur had been cut away. I never did find out why that happened but I remember how pleased we were when that bald bit of me grew back, and I think that was when my fur became a deeper gold.

Do you know, Dear Mary, there is another person in this house? I find him rather exciting, though he doesn't make much fuss of me. I think he must have been away when I first came. He's a young man and Jenny seems to call him 'You Go', while she calls the man 'Darling'. I've discovered that Jenny doesn't really think the black-and-white chap is silly. I've heard her call him by his proper name now — Silvester.

But there's something far more exciting to tell you. Today when we went for our silly-string-walk Jenny told me she was sorry to keep me on a lead but she wanted me to feel safe while I got used to the garden. Then she said, 'Never mind Amber, just another day or two, then I'll let you go free from this horrid thing.' Free! Oh, Dear Mary, if Jenny only knew what I'm thinking of doing. It could be soon now. I'm feeling nervous and excited, both mixed up together.

My purrs are already with you,

love Amber

Dear Dear Mary,

Oh dear, it has all unhappened. Yesterday Jenny promised it would be the last silly-string-walk and I could hardly sleep for thinking and thinking about the next day and coming home. I knew I would have to walk a long way, over many fields, a journey of hours (more than ten) but I felt my dream would help me to find you.

So, when Jenny took me into the garden this morning, as she had promised there was no string on my collar, and when she put me down on the grass I was free, I could start my journey home. Although I was excited I went slowly so that Jenny would not be suspicious. I crept through the first hedge into another garden, then stole forward till I reached a second hedge that reminded me of the one I had hidden in when lost as a kitten. It was then that I started to shake and feel frightened, for on the other side of the hedge was the world-wide field and nothing else I could see except grass and the huge cows. They were looming closer and were more gigantic now than I'd thought when they were further

away. I began to wonder if they would chase me and bounce on me with their feet, heavy as rocks and bigger than plates. I tried to get my whiskers to tell me the way to go, but after the cow field I didn't know.

Oh, Dear Mary, it was spitting-frightening, and I was quivering and trembly. I wanted you so much, to be purring safely on your lap, but I couldn't move. It was not at all like my dream. No Dear Albert to lead me gently on the way, no friendly robin to guide me, I was fixed as stiffly to the ground as a stone, a shaking stone. I'd never felt so unhappy. I was so upset with myself that I could not be brave. Truly, I think it was the most horrid moment of my life.

Then I heard the singing. For a moment I thought it was the Singing Person and my dream was coming true, but the words and the voice were different. 'Ammmber ... Ammmber ... Where are you? ... Not too far ... Ammmber ... Ammmber.' The singing went on and on, and I knew it was Jenny looking for me. Still I couldn't move, but I could hear that she was coming closer, singing with more and more worry in her voice. Then she was there, crawling on her tummy to reach out and stroke me and lift me into her arms, which were trembling as much as I was.

We both shook together and Jenny was crying and saying, 'Oh Amber, I was so worried, I thought you might have run away. Oh Amber, Amber, thank goodness you're safe. Whatever would I have told your Dear Mary if anything had happened to you?'

Then, as Jenny cuddled me, I realised that she does love me very much, and she cares about me and is trying to make me happy. Almost without realising it I began to relax, lying less like a log in her arms. And though I was still trembly I could feel a purr not far away.

Jenny carried me back into the house and up to my room, where she put me on the bed and stroked and stroked me till I stopped trembling. She kept talking and stroking me till I realised that I was purring, first just at level one, but slowly the purr grew and my tail began to waft in the air.

It was so good to be somewhere I knew and with a person I trusted. I shall stay here for the rest of the day, especially as there is fresh milk and I'm weak and tired.

May my loving purrs be with you,

Amber

Dear Dear Mary,

Alas and oh dear, I know now that I can't find my way home to you. I'm not a great explorer after all. I'm not as brave as I thought. I frightened myself nearly whiskerless yesterday. I stayed in my room for the rest of the day and gradually felt better. I've also spent a lot of time thinking about what Jenny said. She was right that it would be bad enough for me if something happened to me, but it would make you yowling sad too wouldn't it, Dear Mary — more bruisingly hurtful than I could bear.

Jenny too would be sad, for after the Unhappening I know that she truly loves me. She came and sat with me many times during the day and slept all night with me, stroking me, talking and singing to me. She even gave me a biggish bit of liver for my supper. I suppose she was trying to cheer me up and I must say I *am* beginning to feel a little more chirrupy.

At least I did try to come to you, Dear Mary, but most of all I know you would want me to be safe, even if I'm not as happy as I was. Also, I was thinking that if you wished me to be safe, then you would not have let Jenny take me unless you trusted her, so I shall do the same and try to settle down and grow to love her, either till she brings me back to you or until this becomes my proper home.

Thoughtful purrings,

love Amber

Dear Dear Mary,

This morning the door of my room was open so I decided to go for a walk in the top part of the house. Your house doesn't have a top part does it Dear Mary? All the rooms are on the ground, so I could jump from any window into the garden. Here I can sit on a sill and see the tree tops, which I like as well. It's a very big house so even when I don't go out there's lots of space for me — so long as I don't meet Lion or Silvester.

I had a sweet surprise while I was exploring, safe in the house this time. I found a new door, which was open, and there was a person sleeping in a bed as big as mine. It was 'You Go', the young man I told you about. He was sleeping very deeply. He was floppy and smelt warmly cuddlesome. So I jumped on the bed and rubbed up close to him, while singing my purring song. He went on sleeping but put out a hand and stroked me, so I settled down and went to sleep beside him for a bit. I used to like it when your family came to visit us, and they had a young man too, but not one who stayed that I could sleep beside. I hope Jenny won't mind or be lonely if some nights I stay with 'You Go' instead of in my room with her.

Happier purrs,

love Amber

Dear Dear Mary,

You will be glad to know that I'm feeling a bit more chirrupy about life here, as I've been left in peace in my camp under the bed, even though the door is open more often. This morning, after Jenny got off our bed, I found my way to the big bedroom which she seems to share with Man Darling, and it's where they drink tea before he disappears for the whole day. In their bedroom I even pounced on her toes, which made Man Darling laugh very deeply.

And I like the balcony attached to the big bedroom. From it I can watch the garden and follow the birds with my eyes, though I felt frightened when Rosie bounced on the lawn and barked loudly. She is a hunter of sticks, which I think is strange. I'd say sticks are very boring to chase. Just lying there on the ground, not running away or fighting back, they aren't even a challenge, and they must be dry and dull to eat.

The good thing about the balcony is that when I get a fright I can rush back inside, through the big bedroom where Man Darling sleeps, and hide in the camp under my bed for a bit before starting to explore again. Jenny told me that Silvester had stomped upstairs and smashed the little round china mat where she puts her night-time water glass. She thought Silvester was cross because she's been shutting the door to downstairs quite a lot to stop everybody else coming up and disturbing my exploring. Silvester is used to going anywhere he wants, so he may have been angry about that, or else just clumsy with those great wodgy feet of his.

I don't mind him and Lion having downstairs all to themselves. I don't like it much down there. Up here is safer.

Purring safely,

love Amber

PS   The bits of liver keep getting smaller. Soon I think there will be none at all, but the biscuits are starting to taste good.

28th May

Dear Dear Mary,

This morning Silvester came into my room and put me off my breakfast. Even though he didn't stay long I had to hide in my camp under the bed. Jenny seemed to sense I was growling upset and she drew me out, pulling out the drawer where I was sitting on the bumps feeling miserable. She cuddled me till I couldn't help purring and then put me and my breakfast on our bed. Then, even though the door was still open I could relax, as Jenny was with me and we'd see Silvester or Lion from high up, if they came in. The biscuits were good and I ate them all.

Afterwards, I went to check out the balcony, but it was raining so much that there were two ducks on the lawn. Imagine liking to get wet and have your feet in water. At least no-one here tries to make me paddle. I'm very glad I'm not a duck. Anyway I must have scared them as they only stayed for a few flicks of my tail.

I met up with Silvester again this afternoon when I was having a roll in the bath. When baths are dry they are purring comfortable to play in. He was on the floor and I could just sense the tops of his ears, peeping. Jenny came in and talked to us both and he went off as if he was bored, but I rushed straight back to the camp in my room, just in case.

Loving purrs,

from Amber

Dear Dear Mary,

How are you? It feels like many moultings since I've seen you.

Yesterday I was very brave. Jenny took me into the garden and I spent five whole minutes creeping on my tummy (just in case) exploring on my own (with her there). I found a dark safe camp behind the shed, where it meets the big holly hedge, and thought I might return to it. Then I suddenly felt frightened and ran through the back door into the house, and upstairs to the camp under the bed in my room, except that on the way I met Silvester and he chased me. But once I was under the bed in my camp I spat at him and he stopped. I just wish he'd realise that it was not my idea to live here, and after all I did try to leave once, didn't I?

This morning Jenny took me outside again and I checked that yesterday's camp was still there. Then I found a wall I like near the back door, where I could rub against the wooden climbing frame the plants grow up. I was just beginning to enjoy myself when Lion came out and rolled around on the ground, and Jenny tickled his tummy and he pretended he was soft and purry. But I didn't like it and felt frightened. Though he didn't even look at me, I know he knew I was there and was telling me that the garden and Jenny are his and that I have no right to be here. But I can't help it can I, Dear Mary?

My purrs are with you,

love Amber

PS As if I did not have enough trouble coping with Silvester and Lion, Jenny must be doing as she promised the vet; the liver finally seems to have stopped. Oh spittams!

Summer 1996

Dear Dear Mary,

My garden camp is wonderful — all dark, prickly and cosy. I don't think Lion or Silvester will ever find me there between the high shiny holly hedge and the back of the little shed-house. One day I stayed there a long time, while Jenny was working in the garden. It reminded me of how I used to sit beside Dear Albert while he made the flowers grow. It was warm here today and felt almost like home, till Lion went by, but he didn't see me.

Do you remember how we would sit, the three of us in the evening, and sometimes I'd sit on your lap and sometimes I'd sit on his? But I didn't stay on his lap when he played loud noises on his long silvery pipe, his saxyphone. You used to tell me that was how you met Dear Albert — you dancing to the music he played with his band of friends. I liked to watch his fingers moving up and down, rather like when I play ping-pong, but I do it quietly. I should have thought (from its name) that people could talk down a saxyphone, but Dear Albert just used to blow and blow, and you said it was all lovely music. Oh well, Dear Mary, I don't suppose even you and I can agree about everything and when it was fast, high and hard it hurt my ears. However, I always thought Dear Albert was fun with the hose-pipe, making the water dance, sprinkling things, and then making his spade go clink-thud in the earth while I watched him.

Lovely remembering purrs,

from Amber

Dear Dear Mary,

Jenny has started leaving me in my garden camp now while she goes out. She was very worried the first time she did it. As soon as her tin can on wheels stopped she rushed to find me, but I was purry and safe. I've made a great discovery since my last letter, Dear Mary. I've found a hole in the wall. It's rather a special hole as it leads back indoors. I get to it from the wall by the gate near my garden camp which is, as you know, behind the shed under the holly hedge.

Inside the house the door to my room is open all the time (that I need it to be) and I think Lion and Silvester have accepted that this room is my safe place. I think it's important that I have territories that are mine, where they aren't allowed. So, now I have two camps, my purring dark one in the garden and the one in my room under the bed. The only trouble is that going from one to the other is twitchy frightening, as I have to travel through Lion country. I hurry-trot with my tummy close to the ground, not looking from side to side. My heart beats in my ears, for it seems a long journey between my room, the way-in-way-out hole in the house wall and my safe camp in the dark of the hedge. And it's no shorter coming back the other way. However, I'm happy in my camps and tomorrow I might try sitting on the sunny wall again — the one by the gate leading to my garden camp.

Loving purrs,

from Amber

Dear Dear Mary,

I can't believe it, Dear Mary, Jenny has left me. She and Man Darling put lots of clothes in some big square bags with handles and went off this morning. I think that is very untrustworthy don't you? Surely she must know that I am still missing you — in fact, if Jenny was going away, why couldn't I come back to be with you?

Fortunately, 'You Go' has not deserted me. He brings me food in my room where I am now a princess, but I also go and sit on him in his room and purr very loudly so I don't get lonely and neither does he. Lion and Silvester are being nicer, especially Silvester. He's not rough and they both leave me to sun myself on the wall or snuggle down deep into my holly hedge garden camp.

People going away is not purring news. Do you remember when Dear Albert had to go away Dear Mary? Oh you did cry, and there was a very big black moving room with many flowers, and I sat by the gate and waited until you came back, all alone except for your young people. Then that evening I sat close to you on your lap and purred my best, as I knew Dear Albert had been poorly for a long time and you didn't like to see his pain, but it was harder with no Dear Albert at all.

Then you told me again how you'd met him when you were a young person at a dance place, where he was playing the big silvery saxphone. Mostly he just used to look at it under the big bed where it lived in its own black house (like a camp I suppose) but it was silvery-shiny when it came out. Sometimes Dear Albert played on it just for us and I liked it when it sounded sad and beautiful all at the same time and made me think of moon-long summer nights when cats sing, calling across the spaces to each other.

There is singing in this house too. It comes from many rooms. 'You Go' has the loud fierce sort. Jenny (when she's here) has quiet, soothing songs, though sometimes they soar screaming high and hurt my ears.

I hope she comes back. I think it is swiping rude and uncaring of her not to think of me. Silvester doesn't like it either when Jenny goes away. We met by the way-in-way-out hole a little while ago and he said not to worry, she always does return. He's beginning to realise that I am lovely, and he himself is not so spittingly bad.

Purrs of love,

from Amber

Dear Dear Mary,

I am missing Jenny rather a lot. It seems a very long time ago that she was here. Rosie doesn't seem to mind too much because she spends such a lot of time with 'You Go'. Dogs are different, aren't they Dear Mary? Rosie gets pleased and waggly about hunting sticks in the garden and actually seems to enjoy travelling in a moving room. She says 'You Go' takes her out exploring in his. It sounds horrible to me. I'd much rather stay here, where it's safe, even without Jenny. Even Lion seems to miss her, though of course he doesn't confide in me. He is a bit quieter, however, and hasn't been much bother.

Silvester really misses Jenny when she goes away, but keeps telling me she always comes back in the end. I suppose it's true, and if it is that's a relief. One thing that has been good is that, because we're both missing Jenny, Silvester has been taking more notice of me. We've been spending some time together and I think we're beginning to be friends, especially now we understand more about each other. He's been telling me the story of how he came to live with Jenny and Man Darling.

He first lived with his mother and his brothers and sisters (but he doesn't know how many) and then he went to be on his own with a family who had rough children. He thinks they didn't mean to be unkind, they had just never had a kitten before. He can't quite remember, but he thinks his name was Pickles then. The house he lived in was one of those where they're all piled on top of each other, he says, though his was at the bottom so that was all right. We think that was why it was called a flat.

Anyway, it had a front door onto the park, which was good, except that the people and the children got bored with Pickles when he wasn't a kitten any more, and used to put him outside, even when it was cold and wet, while they all went off to work and school. They just about fed him, but he said they didn't seem very pleased to see him when he came back in the evening, so he started going further away and having adventures, because the park was good for that. He did bird watching, and hiding in bushes, and it wasn't so bad, and anyway he didn't know any different.

Then one evening, just as it was going deep dark because it was winter time, he came to the edge of the park and saw fine big houses on the other side, so he thought he'd go for a big adventure and explore the gardens he could see in the distance, but he was only half grown-up and not very wise. He saw these huge machines with big lights growling along in front of him, but he thought he could walk between them to the other side of the road where he could have adventures in the beautiful gardens. So he set off into the road, but suddenly he saw a great noisy light rushing at him, and he said it was horrible for all his senses were telling him it would kill him but he couldn't move. It was as if it had power over him, and it roared at him and smashed into him, and then he can't remember anything very properly. It was dark, though he thinks he remembers being lifted gently off the road in kindly hands. But his next clear memory is of a bright light and a man in a green coat, and of feeling poorly and sore all over, especially in his mouth, which was broken, and his leg which was badly hurt too.

Slowly, after many days, he began to feel better, though it was painfully hard for him to eat with wire in his mouth. He lived in a cage. I suppose it was a bit like the one I lived in after I was found in the hedge by the Singing Person, just before you came to take me home Dear Mary. Of course, it was Jenny who came to take Silvester to his new home, where he lived in a cosy room (my room now) for a few days, and Jenny spent lots of time with him, reading books while he sat on her chest.

He says he felt cheerful enough while at the vet's (maybe the same vet I have seen with Jenny) because he knew everyone was trying to make him better. But he felt truly happy once Jenny took him to her home, for she gave him caressing love and a new name — Silvester — as it was New Year's Eve when he came here, which some people call Saint Silvester's Day. He thought it was a good name, much better than his old one, and he says he doesn't even mind when Jenny sometimes calls him 'Silly Cat' because she's been his special person ever since he came here, just as you are still my special person Dear Mary.

Anyway, then he met a sad cat who lived here too. He was called Moses and as soon as they saw one another nose-to-nose, Silvester knew they would be best friends. Moses was so pleased to meet him, for a Terrible Thing had happened some months before. It could even have been the same day that Silvester was born. Moses had had a brother called Aaron, who loved everyone and thought the world was a wonderful place, and that all people were kind to cats. He loved Jenny very much and often asked to be carried around by her like a small person's toy. He also loved Moses very much and Moses loved him, and they did lots of things together, though Moses would roam further afield than Aaron, who always stayed close to home.

One hot June day, when Moses was sleeping in another garden, he felt this fierce bad pain in his head and was shaking all over for many moments. Then he felt cold as cold, even though it was such a hot afternoon. He stayed where he was for a long time because he felt too frightened to move, but he had this heavy feeling that something dreadful had happened. When he came home at last, he found Jenny crying in the kitchen, and he somehow knew that Aaron was dead, so he yowled loud and long, then let Jenny pick him up and cuddle him for a moment, which he never usually allowed her to do.

No-one was ever sure what had happened to Aaron, but Moses thought, because his head was so badly hurt, that Aaron must have been murdered by a big roaring machine, like the one that nearly killed Silvester.

They buried Aaron under the tree where he had often slept in the warming sunshine, and afterwards Moses slept for many hours by him, and was sad as sad. There was another cat who lived here as well, called Nelle, and she was sad too. Moses liked her, but they were not heart-to-heart as he had been with Aaron. Everybody was sad for many months, and Jenny tried and tried to find another best friend for Moses, but with no luck until Silvester was sent to help.

Moses and Silvester became best friends and Moses was happy again. So now Silvester's happy, Moses is happy and Jenny's happy that they're both happy. Moses lived for lots more years until he was very old and cuddly, and so muddly that everyone loved him even more.

What a good story, don't you think, Dear Mary?

Thoughtful purrs,

love Amber

Dear Dear Mary,

Well, she's back. Cool as a raindrop she just walked in with a big green bag and said, 'Hello Amber darling!' Then she wanted to pick me up and cuddle me, but I can be cool too, and I looked the other way and tail-flicked. I do think she should realise that this has not been an acceptable way to behave. I mean, you never left me, well only for an hour or so, and I knew I could wait for you at the gate and be sure that soon you would come back home.

Silvester was quite cheerful about it. He's always cheerful about everything. He says when he had his accident he lost his purr and it took him lots of months and some practising to find it again. It had gone sort of creaky and wouldn't work but he got it going again by chirruping and chirruping till at last it grew back into a proper purr. Now he's found it he never wants to lose it again, so he uses it nearly all the time, and he's good to be with now he likes me. We think there are different levels of purr, starting with just a hardly-at-all purr, when we're not sure whether it's worth it (which we call level one) then moving on through all the other numbers until we reach the rumbly claw-stretching happiness of level ten.

Moses and Silvester

I finally greeted Jenny at about level four, but really I was very pleased to see her, and when Lion came barging in and leaping about he hooked her hand with his claw and bit her for joy. Jenny thought it was funny even though it drew blood from her hand. People take a lot of understanding, for example, Silvester says that just because Jenny and Man Darling go away it doesn't mean they don't love or care about us. Oh Dear Mary, I suppose that's something else I've got to get used to, like I'm having to get used to Lion. He goes everywhere. Nowhere it seems is a No-Go-Lion place, and he loves to sleep on the bed with Jenny and Man Darling, and be in their room where he hopes for milk. Still, if I rush low and quickly through, I can climb into the big, darkly-warming cave cupboard and sleep with all the towels.

However, one day I was sleeping in there and when I woke up, guess who was at the other end — Lion — sleeping as if no cat had ever slept before, which was all right, because he seemed too deeply asleep to notice I was there on my warm patch of blanket. But later he chased me into the kitchen. He's a bully.

Putting-up-with-Lion purrs,

love Amber

Dear Dear Mary,

I've been thinking and thinking, and maybe I am beginning to understand why I'm here. I think you're not well, Dear Mary, for I can remember sometimes it was hard for you to see things. I know people can't see nearly as well as cats, for they can't find their way in the dark like we can. But it was hard for you to see things even in the daytime, not just in the dark, or nearly dark, and that must be trembling horrible.

Jenny is always losing things, especially the glassy bits she puts on her nose to help her see better. You always kept yours on your nose, Dear Mary, but she puts hers down anywhere all the time and then is surprised when she can't find them. It is silly of her, because she needs them to see to find anything, including her glassy bits, doesn't she?

I am truly sorry you are not well, Dear Mary. You always looked after me so carefully. It's not good if it's hard for you to see to make your food or where you can walk safely. I expect you were worried that you could not look after me properly and, because you are so kindly, you did not like to tell me that it was not safe for you to stay in your beautiful house any longer. Oh but it is yowling sad to think of us not living there any more where we had such happy times.

Jenny says she has been talking to you in your new house, which is a huge building but only one small part of it is yours. However, she says kind people are there who help you, Dear Mary, and this makes me glad, but I do wonder why they wouldn't let me live there too. It's strange how kind, thoughtful people can be thoughtlessly unkind all at the same time.

Thinking deeply, and purring,

love Amber

Dear Dear Mary,

How does he do that? I mean, I can jump, of course I can, but I have to concentrate, especially when it's rather high up like the worktop in the warming heart room that has the way-in-way-out hole. I have to wiggle and wiggle before I try it, so anyone can see what I'm about to do. But Lion! Well, one moment he's on the floor and the next he's just sort of there, as if he's floated up, as easy as a bird but with no wings. I've never heard that some cats can fly, but I'm beginning to wonder, for Lion has *powers.* You have to have *powers* to catch squirrels, because they really can fly, not so well as birds who can do it without trees to help, but very well all the same. Squirrels also have very bad tempers and swear a lot at cats. I did not see Lion catch this squirrel but it must have been growling noisily, and they're dangerous, for they can bite viciously. Not content with catching it, by the time I knew anything about his kill he was lugging it heavily through our way-in-way-out hole and onto the worktop. I watched for a moment, amazed, then slipped back to the camp in my room. I didn't think I should get in his way.

Later in the day I heard Jenny find the special present that Lion had brought her. He'd been quite thoughtful as he'd left its feet and tail for her to find in the room where she does all her writing. I must admit it was a magnificent present and I think she was impressed, though she didn't keep it long, but buried it in the garden in a safe place.

I don't know if I'm even more nervous of Lion now I know he has *powers.* I think maybe not, for if he'd wanted to hurt me he could have done so by now, but he can glare as if he'd like to burn me up. However, I did manage to say, 'Good squirrel' to him next time I saw him at a distance across the kitchen, and he said, 'Yep' and flew up onto the worktop near the kettle.

Oh well, Dear Mary, I suppose that's a beginning. I think I might see if I can catch a shrew to give to Jenny.

Loving purrs,

from Amber

Dear Dear Mary,

I forgot to tell you that I do not have to jump up high now to go out into the garden. I thought you might be worried that it was too much of an effort for me. No, two little steps made of wood are fixed to the wall which help me. I usually travel this way, though of course I don't bother on the way back down.

Silvester says that before I came, a white cat lived here called Daisy May. She was beautiful and very proud. He liked and admired her, but then Silvester seems to like everybody. She could fly nearly as well as Lion but never caught a squirrel. She would have worried about her perfect beauty being damaged by its teeth and anyway she was rippling supple like a dancer, not packed with power muscles like Lion. It was sad that after many years she became ill and found the leap onto the worktop too hard, so Jenny had the wooden steps made, which were a goodly help. But Daisy was still ill and Silvester missed her lots when she went away and thinks that's why he found it difficult when he got me instead, so soon afterwards, but he's friendly now.

Silvester remembers when Lion arrived as a tiny kitten, with ears that were bigger than all the rest of him, and straightaway he fell in love with 'You Go' and spent lots of time with him, especially cuddled up in his bed at night. I can't imagine Lion as a tiny kitten but I suppose he must have been once. When he arrived Silvester and his best friend Moses and beautiful Daisy May already lived here. He was not frightened of any of them — well he wouldn't be would he? Moses and Silvester were patient with him but Daisy wouldn't let him ruffle her fur, and would spit and swipe to keep him in his kitten place. I wish I'd met her.

Oh Dear Mary, Jenny is putting clothes into those packing bags. Silvester and I think she's going to leave us again and even Lion looks worried. It's not very grateful is it, for I brought her a lovely shrew yesterday.

Wondering purrs,

love Amber

Dear Dear Mary,

I was right, she's been away. I do think it's too swiping bad, just when we were all beginning to settle down quite nicely. I was a bit cool with her when, after days and days, at last she came back, and I think she was a bit ashamed as she took a lot of trouble to be thoughtful with me. Mind you, she took trouble with Silvester, and even Lion who, despite his *powers*, is surprisingly mardy. I must admit he loves Rosie very much and often rubs round her, though she pretends hardly to notice, which is funny and serves him right. But, do you know, Lion has his own 'Mary'?

You can tell this Mary is a proper cat person as she was very pleased to meet me when I arrived, even coming to talk to me in my room. And she always takes care with me. When she has finished helping Jenny (doing lovely polishy things which smell soothing) Jenny makes her a sandwich before she goes home in her moving room. Inside the sandwich is ham, which is the best flavour of the week, perhaps because it's just a tiny piece. So I always sit with her if I can and she sings to me and we purr together.

However, I don't think this Mary has perfect taste in cats, for she seems to think Lion is the best cat that ever was. She makes such a fuss of him, while he goes ridiculously claw-stretchy and purrs at level ten. Sometimes he even bites her or catches her arm with his paw claws-out. Then there's blood and Jenny rushes to put strong-smelling cream on the arm in case it goes bad. Lion's Mary just laughs and pats him more, as if he was a dog, and he looks soppy. He always remembers which day she comes, which I admit is clever, and he's always in the kitchen to see her — unless he's too busy, of course.

Well, Dear Mary, when Jenny leaves us it's good to know that Lion's Mary will come to visit, and this time when Jenny went away a young man who was not 'You Go', stayed and slept in my room with me, so I wasn't lonely at night. Also, it was mostly sunny so I could enjoy being outdoors, safe in my garden camp behind the shed, or on the warm wall where I can wash myself.

The other goodly thing is that there are two young men who come to work in the garden sometimes. They're very polite to me so I feel I should help them like I used to help Dear Albert. I follow them around and watch, and they talk to me and I enjoy their company when they're being peaceful, only sometimes they make the most dreadful loud noises while doing their work, and I wonder if this is necessary. Gardening should be gentle and quiet. Jenny is always quiet when she does it — when she can be bothered to be at home, that is.

Another quiet thing Jenny does in the evenings is smooth the clean but rumpled clothes, which give off a warm comforting smell, while she and Man Darling watch the moving colours and voices on the big black box. This stands in the corner of the room with the sofa where I once hid from Lion. There's plenty of room on this sofa for me beside Jenny and she likes me to help her. Sometimes I also help to smooth the warm clothes by sitting on them after she's folded them up.

Now she's home again, at last, she seems to have a huge pile of smoothing to do, while the machine in our room — with the warming heart and the way-in-way-out hole — has been swishing and whirring, and the clothes have been enjoying the sun in the garden too. Silvester says it's always the same when she's left us, and it's good because Jenny has so much to do at home when she comes back that she doesn't go out much. Silvester is always cheerful about everything and pounds all over Jenny with his huge big feet whenever he can, but his claws are not wicked-sharp like Lion's and I don't think he's ever caught even a tiny mouse. But I don't like to mention this in case it makes him feel silly!

Chirrupy purrs,

love Amber

PS ... Ham's not nearly so delicious if it hasn't come out of Mary's sandwich. I've tried it when Jenny's given me a bit, but it doesn't taste the same at all.

Dear Dear Mary,

Do you remember I told you that I had caught a shrew for Jenny? This was a plan that needed me to go bravely into further off parts of the garden as there are no shrews or mice near my camp. Since you had my last letter I've been exploring in far-off areas of the garden and have even been out in the field, though not onto the world-wide side. On the other edge of the garden the field seems smaller and, in the distance, is a big green slope with trees on it. This is not a hill, it's too near for that; the true hill is far away across many fields and I would never go there. However, I had been thinking that I should have more territory than just around the way-in-way-out hole and my camp, and being with the young men in the garden helped with that, as I could go safely with them and sit and watch, for Lion goes further afield and has no interest in helping in the garden.

I found some longer grass near the hedge and soon sensed that there were shrews — not many, but a good few if I was patient. All cats know how to be patient when hunting. I waited and waited until there was a quiver and a rustle deep in the grass. I could feel it in my whiskers as well as in my ears. Then I saw the shrew, only a small one, and I was quiet as quiet, and still as still, except for the very tip of my tail which twitched for action. Then POUNCE and I had it. I carried it to my camp and let it go a few times to get it tired. As you know, Dear Mary, cats do not have instantly killing mouths and some prey, such as squirrels, can bite very nastily. But this was only a small shrew so I did not tire it for long, besides there's always the risk that if you play that game too long your carefully caught present can escape, and that's a great waste of time. You see, Dear Mary, hunting has many parts to it if it's done perfectly.

First you must always keep your claws sharp and ready. This was hard when Jenny didn't let me go out, but once I started to explore the garden I soon found a big piece of tree lying on the ground quite near the way-in-way-out hole. Lion and Silvester use it too. In fact, Silvester says it was once a standing-up tree that had big purple sweet-smelling flowers in springtime. All the cats who have ever lived here have loved to satisfy their claw-scratch on its friendliness. Then suddenly it fell over when there was a big wind one night. Everyone was sad and, although Jenny didn't like it squashing all the flowers, she loved the tree too and knew how important it was for us. So when it was cut up she asked the young man, Simon, to put a big piece of it alongside the little path to the grass, to be there for claw-scratching for ever and ever. Now it's known as the important tree and we all use it, and I must admit, Dear Mary, it's the best claw-scratching place I've ever found in my life.

Yes, I always keep my claws sharp for, as well as being necessary for hunting, they're also my protection. Cats sometimes need to rush up trees to escape from dogs and you can't grip to do that if you've neglected your claws. You can also use claws to scratch anyone who comes too close and threatens you. I remember when I was with the Singing Person one of the other cats had to have a little white lump put down his throat, and he struggled and spat and lashed out with his sharp claws and drew blood from the Singing Person's hand. Not that it did him any good as she just laughed and wrapped him up tightly in a towel while her friend opened his mouth and slip-down went the white lump. Then he was cross and had to wash himself to pretend he didn't mind.

I could never scratch a person. I think it's very ungracious. I always go soft and curvy if someone picks me up. At least, usually I do. I suppose if I was frightened I might lie stiff in their arms. Well, yes of course, I did go like a log at the time of the Unhappening. I'd forgotten that, but I would never, ever hurt a kindly person, not even with love pats. Guess who I'm thinking of, who lives here? I don't know how he always gets away with it.

Silvester is so funny sometimes, he makes us all laugh. He thinks it's part of his job. Of course, he keeps the claws on his giant paws sharp on the important tree, but now and again he likes to try them on the side of the sofa. He takes no notice at all when Jenny claps her hands, telling him to stop, nor even when Man Darling gets cross. Once he made a deep growly noise and threw one of those wide papers he disappears behind at Silvester. It fell right near him and flopped and spilt its many wings all over the floor. I felt frightened, and I was safe on the window-sill, but Silvester just looked over his shoulder, chirruped cheerfully and went back to what he was doing!

However, next time it happened, Rosie was in the room, and when Jenny clapped her hands, she rushed across the room barking at Silvester. That stopped him all right! He looked amazed as he jumped up onto the sofa, for Rosie is usually too good a dog to chase cats. Once she'd stopped him she went back to her cushions on the floor. We all thought this was a good game and it happens once every few days, though Silvester wins as he sometimes visits the sofa secretly when neither Jenny, nor Man Darling, nor Rosie are there. As he says, it's only the end of the sofa near the wall which no-one ever sees so, to be honest, he can't imagine what all the fuss is about.

Like me, Silvester would never ever people-scratch on purpose, though he admits that when he settles on Jenny's lap (or her chest in bed) he plays love rhythms on her so deeply with his paws that his claws come out with the pleasure of it. She just says, 'Ouch, Silly Cat,' then lets him pound her even more and puts up with the little red marks. Oh Dear Mary, though I never prickled you, that reminds me again of sitting on your lap — that wonderful, best lap.

Love-kneading purrs,

from Amber

Dear Dear Mary,

I am sorry, I've just realised I was so busy last time telling you all about claws, that I fogot to tell you what happened about the shrew I caught. As I said, there are many parts to hunting, and the last part is deciding what to do with your prey. Of course, you can eat it, like Lion does, but I'm not keen on this, even with mice, and certainly not with shrews which taste bitter. No, I like to give presents, partly because it shows that though I am very gentle most of the time, I am as much a cat as any Lion and my claws are as sharp.

So, I took my shrew and ran floor-low through the kitchen, with a little growl, to make sure Jenny noticed as I carried it into the big bedroom and placed it carefully on the carpet where she couldn't miss it. Soon she came up and was impressed. Well, it was a goodly present and, as she said, it showed I was beginning to feel like a proper cat. She thought I was a clever skilled hunter and made a fuss of me, which was purr-pridening. Mind you, I do think people are odd about the presents we bring them. Jenny buried mine but I expect it was to keep it safe in case she needs to look at it later.

Oh, Dear Mary, she's just been up that ladder into the hole in the ceiling and has brought those threatening bags down again. I'm afraid she must be going to abandon us once more. How horrible.

My loving purrs are with you,

Amber

Dear Dear Mary,

It's hard to believe, but Jenny and Darling have been away again for many days. Even Silvester was surprised at how long they were gone, and I noticed Lion looking lonely. He doesn't really talk to me but doesn't bother me much either. I certainly try not to bother him, but he tells Silvester some secret thoughts because, I suppose, he feels close to him. Silvester must have been like a big brother when Lion moved here away from his own family. But, Dear Mary, he's never known what it's like to be lost, hungry and treated cruelly like I was, or squashed on the road like Silvester. No, Lion's *always* been loved — easy life, lucky cat.

While Jenny was away I explored further afield and will tell you about that soon, but the main news is that, only a few days after she came home, she took me to the vet's. This was yowling upsetting, especially as she did not give me any breakfast. Instead I was put in the basket and bumped around in her tin-can-on-wheels, then, if you please, she abandoned me with all those noisy dogs and strange smells. How could she be so thoughtless? However, she did say she'd come back and there was a nice nurse, but I felt frightened that I might be there forever. When the vet came to see me he talked to me kindly, then stuck a needle in me and I don't remember any more till I was waking up feeling sleepy on a warm blanket. Then, soon afterwards Jenny came to collect me.

I didn't mind the moving room so much this time, now it was travelling in the right direction. Jenny was well pleased to see me and I was fully glad to see her and be back in her house. It was *like* going home even though it wasn't with you. She gave me some food and it was fish, 'For a treat', she said and, do you know, Dear Mary, when I ate it my mouth felt all lovely. When I moved my tongue about a tooth had gone, there was no ache and all my mouth felt light and clean. I hadn't realised that it was bothering me, so he must be a very clever vet to know that he could make me feel so much better. I shall trust him.

Chirrupy purring,

love Amber

PS I chased my tail to celebrate.

Autumn 1996

Amber is right that we were away too much during her first year with us; my husband Graham's work commitments with the International Co-operative Movement took us to four continents. It was only for ten days or so on each occasion, but if you add two weeks' holiday and put all of that into cat time by multiplying by seven, then she had good reason to complain.

The good news, however, is that, to date, we have never had to leave the house without a resident animal sitter of one sort or another. Harry and Hugo, in the way of modern sons, have each in turn been away and then returned to the nest for a while. We have even been able to borrow someone else's son sometimes. Pippa and Ray, who help out generally, have also house-sat for us. The animals have always been fine under all of these regimes, but the cats in particular are thrilled to see us back. It seems a myth to me that claims that cats are completely happy so long as they are well fed and watered, and in their familiar surroundings. For they do miss their main people.

There was a positive outcome from our fickleness though, for it gave Amber the chance to discover young men. She is a people cat, always the perfect hostess to any visitors, making sure that they feel welcome, but she soon realised her penchant for young males of the species. As she grew more confident, loving to be in the garden, a weekly bonus was *when Simon the gardener and his assistant came to work in it. Back trouble keeps me from doing as much as I would like in the garden, but Simon makes up for my failures and Amber soon discovered the joys of keeping him company and being a great help.*

I postponed fundamental treatment to her mouth (which required a general anaesthetic) until she had begun to settle. However, during August I felt we were on our way, and by the early autumn of 1996, for one so nervous, Amber was making good progress. But then in November there was a major glitch for she came close to being run over. This set her back a few weeks, indeed for several months afterwards she would not venture out into the lane at all. Silvester seemed to sense her distress and, being such a good natured chap, made renewed overtures of kindness.

Then came Christmas. This was the cheer-up Amber needed. It was her first Christmas, for Mary, with her particular committed faith, does not keep the festival. Amber loved the rustle and bustle, and helping me to wrap presents, write cards and decorate the tree. Then, on the day itself, there was the wonder of the turkey and the warmth and excitement of being allowed in the 'best' room, with the glow of the coal fire, the allure of velvet and the laps of visitors to grace with her purr.

Dear Dear Mary,

I am feeling sprightly and well, and enjoying my new mouth. Are you all right too? I wonder if you have to swallow white lumps when you have been to see your doctor. After I came home from the Clever Vet's, Jenny had to open my mouth and drop a tiny lump on the back of my tongue which went down my throat. She did this every morning and evening for maybe six days. I didn't like this at all and got to know when she was coming. Well, it wasn't very difficult as she'd say, 'Amber it's time for your pill'. (That's what the white lumps are called.) This gave me time to hide under the table or sofa, but she always got me out, and I'm too polite to scratch or struggle. Then I had a better idea, which was to pretend to swallow the pill and then, when she wasn't looking, spit it out. However, she noticed I was doing this and waited to make sure it had gone, and if it hadn't, she opened my mouth again and was firm that I must swallow the pill. We both tried to be more cunning than the other and I think I might have won, only then the game stopped, so I shall never find out.

As you know Dear Mary, it's important for cats to have safe places and I'm sorting mine out. The top in the kitchen near the kettle is Lion's, but the table in the corner I make my territory, for Jenny puts my food on one of the long seats now I'm braver. I will not let Lion (flying or not) come to that spot. If he tries, I stay still and spit, and he usually takes the hint, though not always.

He doesn't chase me so much elsewhere in the house and garden either — only when Jenny's about. I think he's just showing off then, wanting her attention. Anyway, I try to stay still and make a spit-yowling noise, which frightens me, if not him, it's so loud. It certainly worries Jenny, who always comes running to pick me up and tell Lion he's bad. I think she worries he's hurting me, but the fierce sounds are mine and, though he swipes mightily, his paw is safely far from me. I will tell you what is odd about Jenny though, when she's cuddled me and made sure I'm all right, she then goes and makes a fuss of Lion too. I don't understand her sometimes, do you?

Puzzled purrs,

love Amber

Dear Dear Mary,

It's been lovely warming weather hasn't it? I was sitting in the garden under the window to my room, when I remembered how Lion had climbed up the tree and glared at me through it. I thought, 'I could do that,' so I did, carefully climbing high up the tree until I got to the window, only this time it was open. Next, I moved cleverly from the branch of the tree onto the window-sill and there I was back in that special room, only it looked different. Now, there was a beautiful white cloth, with many tiny holes in it, on the bed, and the door was shut. I would look my best rolling on such a cloth instead of a boring one, which was all I had when I lived in this room. I'm surprised Jenny did not think of this, for she likes me to look beautiful.

Oh, I may not have told you, Dear Mary, that because I'm feeling more at home here now I do not need to go into my room any more, for I keep 'You Go' company on his big bed and help Jenny lots in her work-room. She has many papers in there, as well as her writing machine, and also some comfy sitting places.

At the other end of the house (which is a long way) I go into the deep dark cave of the cupboard and sleep there sometimes too. This is a favourite place for Silvester as well, but he goes on a high-up shelf and I usually choose a cosy box at the bottom, and we both purr contentedly. Once though, I was very deeply asleep when there was a thunderous thump just in front of my nose. It woke me up in less than a moment, but it was only Silvester falling out of the cupboard. He's a dear cat but clumsy because of his accident. He can do most things but he is not graceful like me and he certainly can't fly. So to travel from his high-up shelf, he stretches his front paws onto the rail where the towels live and from there falls onto the floor. It sounds hurtful, but he chirrups cheerily as he lands and goes off elsewhere. I've not seen him climb up to his shelf, but I expect he must have his own system for that too, but I wouldn't tease him, for I actually think he is very brave flinging himself down like that. Besides, he's a good friend.

Anyway, there I was back in my room with no way out. Of course, I could have gone back down the tree, but it's well known that cats are not so comfortable going downwards and I didn't much fancy it. Anyway, if I did that no-one would know how cleverly I'd climbed up.

Shut doors are difficult. I scratched and scratched, but it would not open. Then suddenly, there was a chirrup on the other side. Silvester was saying not to worry, Jenny was bound to come upstairs soon and he would stay to tell her. He wondered though how I'd got into the room. When I told him, he chirruped amazedly. The next moment I heard Jenny asking Silvester why he was sitting looking at the door, so I scratched as loudly as I could, then she laughed and opened it. She looked at me and at the open window. She did a very impressed, 'Oh Amber!' Then she picked me up and cuddled me, and I was purry and proud.

I'm more purry most days now and, as I've said before, have begun to go further afield. I will tell you about that soon.

Adventurous purrs,

love Amber

Dear Dear Mary,

I told you how I was making places in the house entirely mine, where I will not let Lion come. Of course, being a cat underneath his pose of lion, he understands the rules, even though he likes to pretend that he doesn't have to keep them unless it suits him. However, he is useful for keeping the garden territory safe from passing raiders and he does not bother me in my garden camp by the holly hedge, nor on my wall near the way-in-way-out hole into the house.

Once all of that was satisfactory, and there were people to help me feel safe in the garden, I began to explore further. Hunting is good in warm weather and, when I'm absorbed watching for a shrew or mouse, that's mostly all I think about, though, as you know, Dear Mary, cats have many ways to be aware of danger; our whiskers and ears keep listening, even if the rest of us is busy doing something else.

I told you how I caught Jenny a shrew in the long grass where they live, near the corner of the garden with the hedge to the field. Altogether I have now caught three, and given them all to Jenny. There did not seem to be mice there however, which is partly why I went exploring through the hedge and into the field where the cows munch and the slope is on the other side. I would not go into the field until the cows had gone, for although they move slowly they are like mountains on legs close up, and their feet are likely squashers. They are also very untidy, leaving great smelly splats all over the grass where they stand and they do not wash themselves. Cats are neat, with polite manners, which is one reason why people love us so much.

I travelled warily out into the wideness of the field, keeping low, and I reached the slope which has a goodly cover of trees, with my heart beating quicker than quick. It was quiet and I felt safe there, and could hear small mice rustling. When I was breathing more calmly I caught one and went back across the field as fast as I could, but there were no hiding places and my heart was running faster than my legs. So, although it is a good hunting place, and on the other side of the garden from the world-wide field, I don't think I shall go to the slope any more. I was reminded too much of the Unhappening and I began to go trembly. I decided to try again in a different part of the garden and have discovered a few mice there. These will have to do.

Decidedly purring,

love Amber

Dear Dear Mary,

Hunting is fine and important, but sleeping in the sun is even better. I've explored the front way into the garden — past the important tree, then through the hedge into the next garden and along the front of that house. From there it's easy to cross the little bumpy road where the moving rooms travel. Moving rooms are dangerous as I knew even before hearing Silvester's story, so I go very carefully, and you can hear when they are coming from a long way off, so don't worry Dear Mary.

On the other side of the bumpy road is a wonderful high wall with flowers underneath — lots of those that you and Dear Albert used to have in your garden, which cats love to chew and roll on. (Jenny has some near my garden camp, but not enough.) This is such a perfect place to purr. At least I thought it was until suddenly I heard a room-on-wheels coming backwards towards where I was basking. I was too frightened to move but it was only going slowly and passed me safely. Then it joined the main part of the bumpy road, turned itself round and grundled off. I stayed where I was and all was quietly perfect again for a long time. Much later it came back, slowly turned the corner and passed my basking spot again. Lying deep in the flowers I was not so frightened this time and have decided I can safely stay there even when a room-on-wheels goes by.

There's also a beautiful garden on the other side of the bumpy road, with many good sleeping places under bushes. Miss Bluebell lives there. She's smokey-blue with golden eyes more round than round. She's elegant — proudly aloof — but is kind enough not to mind me being in her garden.

On the side of my own garden there's the field with the slope and the small house where the moving rooms live when they're not moving. They seem to need to rest too. I know now when it is Jenny's that's coming (for every moving room has a different grundle) and I often go to meet her on the rough stones called the drive. Silvester knows the sound too and Lion is far too clever not to be there first, except that he's often too busy in far-away territories. One day though, he arrived just as I got there to say 'Hello' to Jenny. His glare was unmistakable, 'I'm meeting the car, okay?' So I went to wait in the garden, which was nearly as good, and at least he's told me the name 'car' which is shorter to write.

Loving purrs, from Amber

Dear Dear Mary,

Yesterday it was raining. Suddenly! How unkind, after all these purr-warming days. Big, cold, plopping drops. We were none of us pleased. I delayed going out as long as I could. I waited and waited, watching from the kitchen window, willing it to stop, but it kept on drip, drip, dripping.

I complained to Jenny, for people can sometimes be clever and helpful, and I wondered whether, if she tried forcefully, she could make the rain stop. To be fair to her, she understood what I was saying, but explained that this was not something she could do. Then I had an idea; maybe it wasn't raining everywhere. So I went to the way-in-way-out hole and looked out through it. But it was still raining. Then I went to the door that opens onto the garden near the kitchen and asked Jenny to check for me. But it was still raining. I sat by the open door and watched the miserable water falling, splashing wetly, and I willed it to stop, but nothing happened, even though I twitched my tail more and more crossly.

However, I would not give up, so I moved upstairs to Jenny's writing room and her comfortable wide window-sill. I glared and glared at the persistently dripping water, but still it did not stop. Feeling more and more fed up, I made my way to the main door — the one which opens onto the front path, the one where Jenny and Darling and 'You Go' jingle their keys when coming in. I had to wait a long time until Jenny was passing. 'Oh Amber you don't give up do you?' she said, laughing a little, though I could not see what was funny, especially as my determination worked, for when she opened the door ... yes ... it had stopped raining.

Jenny and I were both impressed. It was most satisfying and proves that it does not rain always at every doorway. I gazed out, purring at the dry air before I went out to scrabble in the wet earth.

Pleased purring,

with love,

Amber

Dear Dear Mary,

How disappointing. I'm wondering now about my theory, for although I was able to be in the garden for a good hour after I'd stopped the rain by glaring at it from this window and that door, it began again later in the day, and now I'm afraid to say that the rain is winning, falling at every door and window no matter how long I wait, or how fiercely I glare or lash my tail. Oh spittams!

Sleeping in the sun outside is not often possible, but as you know there are many goodly places in the house to sleep comfortably, especially in the cave which is the cupboard with all the towels in it. Silvester and I are often in there together. He has his own shelf and I have mine, but Silvester and Lion both think that the best purring sleeping place is the basket near the way-in-way-out hole. It lives on the warming heart that throbs and hums for hours in the day. Sometimes the basket has clothes in it which makes it claw-stretchingly comfortable. Lion and Silvester use it often, sometimes even sharing it together, which is a squash for both of them, but then they are close friends. Maybe one day I shall be allowed to have a turn. I hope so.

You will remember Dear Mary, how pleased I always was to meet your friends. Well, Jenny has friends too. They come to the house and sit and talk, and eat and drink, then talk some more. As you know, I think it's important to make visitors feel happy to be here, and I take this job seriously. As soon as they sit down I make sure they are comfortable by rubbing round them and sitting on their knee for a while. Jenny says she's never had a cat who is such a welcoming hostess and this is pridening, especially as it comes naturally to me and does not require any effort, though it is right to keep practising these skills.

Of course, Silvester and Lion will sometimes call by to talk to visitors, but they don't know how to take trouble like me. By the way, I have found out something interesting about Lion; he is not quite as brave as he thinks he is! I have my biscuits on the long seat at the table in the kitchen. Lion and Silvester are given theirs in the warming heart room near the way-in-way-out hole, but I have my own space for eating which makes me feel safe, and even Lion respects this — most of the time. Once he did try to come near, but I spat at him and he took the hint, though this does not mean that he will never chase me in other places! Silvester says that I mustn't take him too seriously and it is true that he's never actually hurt me.

Anyway, what I was going to tell you is that yesterday I was sitting quietly on the table and Lion was on the worktop close to the kettle, when 'You Go' came into the kitchen in a hurry and snatched up something he'd forgotten. It was a swift rushing movement, but Lion was swifter, for he was scared whiskerless. He leapt wildly from the worktop to the doorway in one huge flight and vanished through the way-in-way-out hole, not to be seen for a long time. I watched amazed as 'You Go' paused to say, 'Oh dear, sorry Bernard, it's only me ...' before disappearing through the main door. I didn't find 'You Go' rushing out frightening at all, and thought it was funny that Lion, of all cats, should be upset so easily.

Silvester chirruped into the kitchen, relaxed as ever, and I let him sit with me on the table. It's reassuring to know that Lion has his twitchy side. Silvester says Lion is extra frightened of dogs as well, so that when the Gentle Mother comes with bouncing Bruno, Lion is yowling upset. Silvester and I just keep away from the rooms where Bruno is, but Lion goes trembly, even though Bruno is all noise and no bite. But when Lion was not very old, at something called Christmas, Bruno bounced at Lion while he was on Jenny and Darling's bed and, instead of sitting and spitting, he panic-ran and Bruno bounced yippering after him. Lion never forgave him nor any other dog that is not Rosie. Rosie he adores rubbingly, but she is family, even though she can be a loud barker.

Braver-than-Lion purrs,

love Amber

Dear Dear Mary,

Jenny and Darling's bedroom is purring popular with all of us. Silvester usually sleeps on Jenny and, if he's not too busy on his nightly prowlings, Lion sleeps near Darling's feet, who too often puts clothes in a packing bag and takes it away somewhere for one night or more. When this happens Rosie does not like Jenny to be lonely, so she sleeps on Darling's part of the bed, though as she sleeps sideways, not up and down the bed, she takes up much more room than Darling, so Jenny only gets a squeezed space perching on the edge. Silvester also makes sure she has plenty of company by pounding on her head or sleeping on top of her, with Lion moving in closer too. She keeps water by her bed in a tall pool of glass, which Silvester thinks is a lapping-good idea. He likes to drink from it but when Jenny noticed him doing this she realised he needed his own water supply. So now there are two glasses placed beside her — one with a lid, which is hers, and a private pool for Silvester, which makes him more cheerful than ever.

I often sleep in the cave, but in the mornings, when Lion has gone, I sometimes sit in the doorway between the cave room and the big bedroom and watch, for when Jenny and Darling wake up they make hot tea and they drink and drink. How do people's mouths not get burnt? And they talk and talk for many minutes before properly getting up. But first, while the kettle is whispering to itself, Jenny goes downstairs to fetch Rosie and then they're all cosily on the bed together. It looks purring merry and I hope one day I shall be able to join them, but I don't like to go there yet, as it's one of Silvester's special times. I'm beginning to feel more settled though, mostly thanks to Silvester who is chirruping

friendly, but I don't think I should go pushing in, do you, Dear Mary?

More contented purrs,

love Amber

PS Jenny has been more settled too. She's not abandoned us lately and that *is* good.

Winter 1996

Dear Dear Mary,

Something so spitting horrible has happened that I can still hardly bear to think about it, which makes it yowling hard to tell you, and that's why you've not heard from me for such a long time. I'm still very shaky and upset, and Jenny has given me a tray to use, so that I don't have to go out if I don't want to. I shall certainly not go far, not ever again.

As you know, Dear Mary, I had become quite brave, crossing the bumpy road, sleeping in the flowers under the high wall (when the weather was warm) and visiting Miss Bluebell's garden. I was beginning to go all round the house and enjoy having my own special places, like the long bench-seat in the kitchen and my shelf in the cave. I liked helping Jenny with her writing work and her visitors. In fact I was feeling very much happier altogether.

But then the bangs started. Mostly they were far away, and I had heard them before, when we were living together, Dear Mary. Anyway, one day when it was not very late and I was just coming back from Miss Bluebell's garden, there was a huge big bang so near me that my whole body went on end and I ran with all my might, not thinking of anything but being safe in the house. I forgot about all the other dangers and, as I crossed the bumpy road, something thundered, roared, hit and tossed me, and I rolled and rolled in all the dusty dirt. Oh, Dear Mary, I just ran and ran, in through the way-in-way-out hole, straight upstairs, into the room where 'You Go' sleeps and under his bed. I did not really know where I was going, I was too frightened. Then I just shook and shook, but at least I knew I was safe.

Jenny was out when the Terrible Thing happened so no-one missed me until the next morning, by which time I had nearly stopped shaking but felt all stiff and bruised. I didn't want to come out from where I felt safe, but Jenny came looking for me. She began to worry when I didn't appear for breakfast. She was glad when she found me and tried singing to help me come out but, although I very much wanted to be cuddled and comforted, I couldn't move. It was as if my paws were clawed into the carpet forever. Then Jenny, who was lying flat on the floor, reached her arm under the bed until she could touch me, and she could tell I was stiffly-trembly all at the same time. 'Come on Amber darling,' she said so kindly, and then she somehow got hold of me and dragged me out despite my claws being stuck in the carpet. Once she was holding and stroking me I did feel a bit better, and she soon realised I was hurting, for my beautiful fur was dirty and lumped up in a place near one of my hind legs.

I was not very happy about what happened next though, for she put me in that basket and took me off in her moving room. I would rather just have stayed cuddled up to her, but I must admit it hurt me to be held. Jenny said it was important to check, for at the very least I was in shock, which is yowling dangerous. Of course, she did not know what had happened to me, but the Clever Vet examined me and had a good guess, saying I had been 'rolled' by a car. Fortunately, nothing was broken anywhere but he knew I was hurting in many places and he touched me gently. Even though he stuck a needle in me I forgave him because I knew he was trying to help — and so was Jenny.

When we got home, she took me back into my own room, brought me food and warming milk, and said I should stay there resting quietly until I felt better. She took the beautiful white cover off the bed and gave me my old cover, which was sensible as my claws might have caught in the holey lace. And anyway it was comforting, like an old friend.

After Jenny had stroked me and talked to me for a little while, and I had lapped a little milk, she left me on my own. I went into the darkness under the bed and sat on the lumps Jenny keeps there for presents. I began to feel more peaceful as I could feel the quietness round me and sensed all the safe house noises. They came through the floor and I knew them all and it was good. I slept deeply-deep and when I woke up I felt hungry and ate a little food. Jenny peeped in to see if I was okay and, although I wasn't yet, I managed a small purr (about level two) and she was pleased.

I stayed in my room all that day and all night, not wanting to do more than rest and sleep, and feel safe. Next morning, when Jenny brought my breakfast she found I was asleep on the bed instead of under it, so she guessed I was feeling better. Silvester came in with her and was very kind. I was still too upset to tell him exactly all about the Terrible Thing but, as I have said, he is far from silly and knew something dreadful had happened to me.

Don't worry too much Dear Mary, I shall tell you more soon.

Lowly purring, love as ever, Amber

Dear Dear Mary,

I'm much better again, but am going out hardly at all. Two days after the Terrible Thing happened Jenny left the door to my room open so that I could leave it when I felt ready, and Silvester could visit. He chirruped in and was very understanding and kindly. Of course, he knows what it's like to be in shock and how easy it is for a car to be roaring in the wrong place when a cat is coming the other way. He said I shouldn't worry as Jenny would look after me and I would get completely better. After all, he'd been nearly squashed dead and look at him now.

Of course, Silvester is different from me. Nothing seems to worry him or upset him here. It's his belonging place and Jenny is his person, whom he trusts to his last whisker. That was the way I felt when I was with you Dear Mary, though as you know, I've always taken life nervously. No-one could say that of Silvester though, for him it's just one big chirrupy purr.

Anyway, slowly I began coming out of my room, first going into the big bedroom, then hiding deep down in the cave. Next I went downstairs and when I met Lion he actually said, 'You okay?' I was so surprised I only just managed to answer, 'A little more myself, thank you,' before he floated up onto the worktop by the kettle, saying as he flew, 'Better be careful, Goldie, cars is dangerous. Worse than me!' Then he grinned wickedly as he hooked Jenny with his claw, asking for milk.

I must admit, Dear Mary, everyone has been surprisingly kind. Always friendly, Rosie came to my room several times. I'm sure it was to see how I was and not just to check if there was any food to finish up. Then yesterday, for the first time I went out through the way-in-way-out hole, just as far as my wall and for a quick scrabble nearby. It was good to feel the air and earth again, but I didn't stay out long. Jenny has moved my tray downstairs now, near the sploshing and whirring machine into which she puts cloths and clothes before hanging them up in the garden. This is also near the helpful steps leading to the worktop near the way-in-way-out hole. This was thoughtful, as it means I need only go out when I choose.

Purring more strongly,

love Amber

Dear Dear Mary,

I'm feeling a little better but hardly going out, for when I do, I go trembly and am glad to come back in again. It's also gone cold outside now and this is never my favourite time of year. It's good to return to my room, or find 'You Go' and sleep on him in his room, or slumber restfully in the warmth of the cave.

One morning, when I came out from the cave, Silvester was sitting by the whispering kettle while Jenny had gone downstairs to fetch Rosie. I knew they would all be getting back on the bed once the tea had been made, and Silvester said why didn't I come too. It was surprising and kind of him, but then he has been most concerned about me and the Terrible Thing. Anyway, there we all were on the bed, Jenny, Darling, Rosie, Silvester and me. Jenny and Darling were pleased to see me on the bed. They thought I was brave and made a big fuss of me. Rosie took up the most room. Silvester pounded first on Darling then on Jenny with his huge paws, while I sat quietly purring somewhere in the middle.

Now I go on the bed quite a few mornings, though not always, for it would not be fair on Silvester who is so kind to share his purring merry treasure with me. Though I do not go every day it's such a help to know that I can go on the bed like this whenever I wish (once we're sure Lion has gone off). It's what I call a *rare mouse*, which means a special claw-stretching treat. It gives me a deep feeling of belonging and I'm grateful to Silvester, who's a dear chap.

Better-purring love,

from Amber

PS Jenny is starting to do interesting but strange things!

Dear Dear Mary,

As I said, Jenny is behaving strangely. The first thing I noticed was that she took all the bumps out from under the bed and started looking at each one and writing about them in a little book. Then she put them in small piles round my room and brought in several rolls of brightly-coloured paper, which she left in another heap.

Also, she's been spending many, many hours writing and writing on the kitchen table as if she is writing tens and tens of letters. She takes coloured pieces of card out of packets, then writes on each of them before putting them in white covers. Then she writes some more on these, so she knows where they are going. Oh, Dear Mary, but there are masses and more of them! I've never known her to keep still for so long and not go out hardly at all. This has been happening now for two or three days.

Next, she went up to the big bedroom, which was interesting as she opened the hole in the ceiling and those silvery steps came down. I wondered who lived up there, but it just seemed to be the steps and lots of boxes. She shut Silvester out of the bedroom while she was disappearing and re-appearing up and down the ceiling hole. He sat chirruping cheerfully out on the landing, even though he likes to go up the silvery steps himself and explore under the roof. He tells me it's exciting as you can hear birds' feet above and sometimes they are cooing daftly. When he's been up there before, he's teased Jenny by hiding and pretending he didn't want to come down. He thinks it's funny, but I'd worry, like Jenny, about a cat being trapped up there. I was certainly not feeling brave enough to try any such exploring and was happy just to peep out of the cave to get an idea of what was happening.

Soon Jenny had many big boxes all over the room and when she'd covered nearly all the floor with them, she closed the hole in the ceiling and the silvery steps disappeared. Then she let Silvester chirrup into the room and he was even more cheerful than usual for, as he explained, this was only the beginning of something special, called Christmas.

Suddenly, from downstairs there was fierce barking from Rosie, who then growled angrily, which is not like her at all, but Jenny just laughed, and so did Silvester, for they know that Rosie hates anything to come in through the main door when it's shut. There's a hole in the door covered by a shiny flap. It's probably a tail's length wide and a long whisker high. I believe it's called a letter-box and I think you had one too Dear Mary, but I never took much interest in it as it was quiet and never caused much fuss. This one does, for when the man comes with the letters and puts them through it, Rosie is aroused like a snarling wolf! She attacks them as if they were deadly rats and shakes them grippingly, so that many of them have holes made by her biting teeth. So the tens and tens of letters which fall through the shiny flap each day are driving Rosie mad and making her bark wildly.

Later ...

There's much rustling about the house. Jenny spends lots of time crackling paper in my room, turning all those bumps into parcels to be presents for people. Now she's finished writing for hours in the kitchen, she goes out for shortish times and comes back with more parcels, which she takes out of many bags, then wraps these in the coloured paper, turning them into presents too. It's a lovely time for me as we're in my room together. Jenny has music and me to help her. Silvester chirrups in now and again, but fortunately Lion doesn't do gift wrapping.

Purring helpfully,

love Amber

Dear Dear Mary,

I forgot to tell you last time, that as well as wrapping and rustling and cooking, Jenny is slowly sorting the boxes that came from the ceiling, and there are all kinds of sparkly dangles in them. Each day Jenny takes out a few and hangs them here and there, so that, gradually, the house is becoming 'Christmassy' as Silvester describes it.

As I said there are tens and tens of letters arriving and annoying Rosie. They all have coloured cards inside and I half wondered if they are the same ones Jenny has been writing for all those hours, coming back to her, though I couldn't see the point of that. Then I realised that Jenny seemed too pleased and surprised with them for that to be the explanation. She would tell me who they were from, 'Oh look Amber, this is a pretty card from Ian and Angela' or 'This is an unusual one from Australia'. So they were not the same ones returning to her; in fact Silvester thinks they come from many friends who live far away. Certainly Jenny likes pinning them on the long logs on the ceiling downstairs, or sticking them all over the doors in the house, which has a special feel to it now, as if something wonderfully purry is about to happen.

All of this is helping me to feel more cheerful, though I hardly go outside and still need to spend time in my room peacefully — or not so peacefully if Jenny is with me and is rustling around.

Not only are coloured pictures popping up on ceilings and doors, but little lights have appeared on strings in many places, some draped on twigs in a big jug in the hall, others at the window under the tree I once climbed to get into my room, and two sets in the room with the talking picture box. I go in that room just a little again now, to be with Jenny and Darling. As you know, my courage has been crouching low for a lengthy time after the Terrible Thing (worse than after the Unhappening) but the Christmassy excitement is helping me feel more myself again.

Fascinated purring,

love Amber

Dear Dear Mary,

Well, this was puzzling. Today, Darling brought a tree into the house. Now, I know you used to bring flowers indoors, and even small plants in pots, and Jenny does the same, for she loves flowers too. But fancy trying to grow a tree indoors. What will happen if it grows through the ceiling? For he has put it in the room with the lowest one of all the rooms in the house. I thought it was most unsensible and that Jenny would tell Darling to take it out again, but not at all, she was delighted with it. She said it smelt of fresh pine (which was true) and then she wrapped silvery paper round the pot. The lowest room in the house is also the velvety room, where I have hardly ever been for the door is usually kept shut. It's also the best room for cats because of the smoothly-soft chairs and sofas, and thick carpets. I wonder why Jenny does not realise this and leave the door open all the time for us to go in and enjoy ourselves.

Anyway, she is purring taken with the tree growing in there, and when I asked to join her she soon heard my scratching and let me in. Oh, Dear Mary, we did have a lovely time. First she wound little lights on strings all through the branches and they sparkled like stars in a dark green sky. Then carefully, one by one, she took silvery, gold and red dangling balls from boxes and hung them on the branches, where they swung, tempting me to pat them, which I did once or twice, and all the time there was pleasant singing music playing soothingly. The tree looks so beautiful now it is what Jenny calls 'dressed' ... and perhaps all those dangles will slow down its growing.

After talking to Silvester ...

I suppose I should have worked this out for myself. The tree is called a Christmas tree and will only live indoors for a few days. After that it will be taken out into the garden to get on with its growing there. Meanwhile, Jenny keeps piling rustling parcels in a heap that is growing much faster than the tree could ever do. There is so much to understand about Christmas isn't there?

Purring more happily,

love Amber

Dear Dear Mary,

Well, now I know about Christmas and it has many days. It began properly when Jenny did a lot of cooking and laid a beautiful lacy cloth on the table, with sparkling glasses and bright silvery knives and forks, in the room with the long logs on the ceiling. (Jenny calls them beams.) That evening, just after Darling came home, two young people also arrived. Jaz and Lakh are part of the family too, so I'd met them before. 'You Go', Jenny, Darling, Jaz and Lakh all had a jolly laughing meal in the long-logs-ceiling room. Then everyone gathered in the velvety room by the fire and the heap of parcels, and the growing tree shone as brightly as it could. It was a purring happy time. I sat on everyone's knee in turn, but made a special fuss of Jaz and Lakh because, although family, they were like visitors, having a house of their own in a faraway place called Didsbury.

I helped them unwrap a huge parcel, which, underneath its rustly paper, was a big basket to put clothes in before they are washed. I thought they should have this basket tested and I'm glad to say that, not only did it feel deeply comfortable, but everyone said I was clever to explore it. Silvester came in for a little while to say 'Hello', but he was so glad to see that I was enjoying myself he soon left, letting me have the velvety evening all to myself. Our visitors were pleased to have my help and, when they left, they carried lots of other parcels away with them in their big new basket, and everyone was saying 'Happy Christmas'. I realised afterwards, though, that the heap around the growing tree had not got any smaller, because Jaz and Lakh had brought many parcels with them, which they'd added to the pile!

The next day was the Eve of Christmas and Jenny was very busy. She spent all day at home cooking and in the afternoon the Gentle Mother came and sat at my table in the kitchen and helped Jenny by listening to singing music with her, while chopping up many potatoes and pulling leaves off little round green vegetables called sprouts. I helped by purring to her as she sat, and tasted a little piece of the pie which she ate with a glowing amber-brown drink in a pretty glass. Later, Big Harry arrived with his special friend, who thinks I'm lovely, and they are sleeping in my room, which is cosy. Jenny was happy to have the house busy with her family, and I could feel gladness all about, which gave me much healing.

Christmas Day came quietly, with Jenny laying the table beautifully again and nose-warming scents of cooking. Rosie wore a bow on her collar and was excited to have Big Harry, his special friend (who is called Rachel) and 'You Go' all in the house together. Then, when Darling had collected the Gentle Mother there was even more excitement, because her dog Bruno was with her and he rushes about making loud yelping noises when he is happy. Darling took him and Rosie for a walk up the field, which helped, but then he was in the house until the evening, so I sort of missed that part of Christmas. So did Lion, who hates Bruno, and even Silvester thought it was best to stay quietly in the basket on the warming heart. I say I missed Christmas, but even though I was up in the cave I could feel the house was happy and it was good.

Later, when the Gentle Mother and Bruno had gone home, I tried some meat called turkey for the first time and it was deliciously tasty. Jenny laughed at how quickly I gobbled it up, purring at level nine. Lion had been grabbing interested when the turkey first arrived and wanted to visit it in the cool garden room, but after it was cooked and Jenny gave him some, he said, 'No thanks'. Typical!

All the family had a happy evening and ate some more, and then the young people all went out and it was quieter. Jenny came and found me in the cave and took me down to the velvety room, where Rosie was asleep in front of a warmly glowing fire. I stayed and purred on Jenny's knee and Silvester chirruped in too, but not Lion, because I think even the lingering smell of Bruno was enough to keep him huffily away. That night I slept better than on any night since the Terrible Thing.

The next day was called Boxing Day. This must be because there are so many boxes, and so much paper left over from the Christmas presents which all has to be cleared up. Some goes in big sacks, and some is burnt by Darling in the garden with Rosie helping him. It was a quieter day with everyone going out for walks (which pleased Rosie) and Jenny did hardly any cooking at all. Everybody ate up the food from yesterday's feast and we had more delicious turkey. The fire was lit in the velvety room and, when the walking was done, I joined Jenny and Darling as they read their books cosily.

Unfortunately, by the evening Darling was looking as white as cooked fish and was feeling coldly-horrible. Jenny made him lie on the sofa with pillows and covered him up with a snuggly blanket, which was a good idea as I could sit on him and help to keep him warm. Jenny said, 'Poor Darling, it's happened again. It's when you stop it all catches up with you'. So Darling being ill is obviously part of Christmas.

Next day he was in bed all tucked up, sleeping and having hot drinks while I kept watch on him from the cave, when I wasn't in my room with Big Harry and Rachel, or with 'You Go' in his. As it happened, on the next morning 'You Go' went away carrying a big packing bag to somewhere called Skiing. Meanwhile, Darling was busy being ill in bed and Big Harry and Rachel were still with us, being good company and taking Rosie for merry walks. There was also still some turkey to eat up and a goodly feeling. I hope Christmas lasts a long time.

Contented purring,

with love from Amber

1997

During 1997 Amber started to settle in properly. For although she and Bernard (Lion as she calls him) continued to disagree, she grew less afraid of him and began to stand her corner. She was helped in this by her strengthening relationship with Silvester and by my accepting some regression following the November 1996 trauma. Prior to that, I had thought Amber had progressed beyond the need to have 'her room' all to herself. Thus, the delicate white lace bedspread had taken its rightful place on the bed once more and the old towels had been removed from the brocade chairs. However, as Amber herself has related, when she was so distressed by the incident in the lane, the room reverted to being covered up, and once again became her safe haven, until, that is, we had visitors early in 1997, one of whom was not only allergic to cats but also a little phobic.

A month or two after all this, when Amber had decided for herself that she no longer favoured the spare bedroom, she was, along with the other two cats, very interested in the temporary resident in that room. A gorgeous, fluffy black, cheery character, this tiny kitten had arrived, as if by parachute, in an elderly lady's so-called cat-proof garden on Chester Road in Macclesfield. She had kept him for a few weeks, but now needed to find him a home and I must admit that I was sorely tempted, but greater love hath no sister ...

Down in Essex, in early December 1996, my sister Sheila's beloved Wallace, brother to Gromit, had been killed on their quiet road at just six months old, on the very day of a family party to celebrate our mother's 80th birthday. Wallace was black with a thick sleek coat. Adorable, partly because he was so unworldly wise, he had obviously failed to learn in time, the danger of cars. Sheila and the family were devastated. Gromit pined, while attempts to find a suitable replacement had, until now, proved unsuccessful.

It seemed that the parachutist, who had to be a survivor of the first order, had been sent to help. I chauffered him down to the rendezvous with my sister, though he escaped from the cat basket en route and spent the rest of the journey sitting contentedly on my knee. This, we soon realised, was typical behaviour. Cheerful, unfazed, bold, adventurous but streetwise, the kitten, now named Chester, was a huge success in his new home, which was just as well, for I think he would have disrupted the balance of personalities in our household, very much to Amber's disadvantage.

She, meanwhile, was to have a special visitor that summer, a visitor whom she found hard to believe was there, so much so that, after taking this key person home, which must have taken about an hour, I returned to find Amber still sitting bemused on the garden seat which we had all shared together. She appeared to be convincing herself that the afternoon's events had not been a dream.

Dear Dear Mary,

Christmas has disappeared. Big Harry and Rachel have gone away. They stayed until this year had started, but now they've gone back to a place called Bright-On, which sounds sunny. A few days later Jenny started taking down all the coloured pictures and the little lights and, well, everything that had given the house its Christmassy feel. I thought it was rather sad, but I helped her, especially as I still didn't want to go outside much.

The growing tree looked empty when all the dangles had gone, carefully repacked into bags and boxes, which then went back through the hole in the ceiling in the big bedroom. Darling then carried the growing tree outside, for Jenny said it would be happier in the cold air. Apparently, unlike dogs and cats who are stretching-happy by a fire, trees do not like warmth and dryness. So I expect our growing tree will stretch its cooling needles joyfully up to the dampening sky. We must all have our special care that suits each of us, mustn't we, Dear Mary? I think that's why you needed to move from our home. Certainly, we all need to feel safe, and slowly this feeling is coming back to me. I feel more cheerful again, though I still do not go far outside, and I still need the comfort of my room sometimes and all the thoughtfulness Jenny gives me.

The house has been having a big clean, which is noisy, with the howling machine grinding through all the rooms. Jenny has put green leaves, and flowers called daffodils, all round everywhere. They are magical, for one day they are green and thin, and the next they have burst into bright yellow flowers like sunshine, which makes me think of the warmer weather and enjoying the garden again — one day when I do not go trembly outdoors any more.

As I've said before, Silvester has been most kindly since the Terrible Thing and today, when I came back through the way-in-way-out hole he was purring in the basket on the warming heart and asked if I'd like to join him. It was the first time I'd ever been in the basket. It's the place that all cats love best. Certainly Lion often has it to himself and he takes up too much room to share it comfortably with anyone for he is rippling-solid. Not that he would say 'No' to Silvester, who thinks life is one big chirrup and, when you think like that, I do believe it makes good things happen. I wish I could be less nervous, but we can all only be as we are.

Anyway, it was purring cosy in the basket with Silvester and he says I can climb into it whenever I find it empty. He calls it the first-come-first-comfy basket and it's good to know that I can add it to my safe places, especially as from there I can keep an ear and eye open to the world outside, and this is slowly helping me to feel more confident again about going into the garden.

Safely purring,

love from Amber

Dear Dear Mary,

Three days ago something happened to the warming heart. It suddenly stopped and everywhere went cold. Neither Jenny nor Darling could make it go again. This meant that the basket has not been cosily attractive at all, for it was surrounded by horribly biting air, and even the cave was not warm. In fact nowhere was warm anywhere in the house, and Jenny, Darling and 'You Go' wore heavy clothes to try to stop shivering. They also put some boxes on wires in some places in the house. These made a bird-wing whirring sound and puffed out some warming air, but not so much as the glowing fire in the velvet room. I thought we should all have gone and lived in there!

Then a man came and worked for many hours. He took the warming heart away and replaced it with a new, shiny one. This one was only half the size of the old one, but fortunately the basket still fitted on top, though it looked a bit wobbly. Soon the house was cosy and warm again, and we were all delighted. At least we thought we were, until we realised that something was different in the warming heart room. Even Lion mentioned it, 'Brrr, cold,' he said. It seems that this new so-called warming heart is so busy warming the rest of the house that it's forgotten the most important part of all, our room. By now we were all fed up and Jenny was not pleased either, as the clothes were not drying where she hung them up because of the howling wind coming through the way-in-way-out hole. We all hoped she would do something about such a serious situation, but meanwhile something else unsettling happened.

We had visitors to stay for one night. As you know Dear Mary, I think it is important to make people who visit us feel welcome, and I take a lot of trouble over this. These were stroking kindly people too, or so I thought. The woman visitor said I was lovely and made a big fuss of me, although the man visitor seemed a little nervous of me — yes, of me, really! He was quiet and I liked him. I tried to tell him that I was not at all frightening, by purring against him but, although I tried my best, I could sense he had that stiff feel that cats get just before they go trembly. I thought I should continue to reassure him and, as they were sleeping in my room I was glad to share it with them. I was looking forward to purring on them all night, for surely by then the man would know I was his friend. But when I followed them into my room the woman gently picked me up, put me on the landing and closed the door — the door to my room. How could she?

For a while I was so shocked I just sat there and thought. After a little I decided to act by scratching politely at the door, but they took no notice. I thought some more, then scratched a little louder, but still they took no notice. I tried a third time, louder still, and still they took no notice. By now I was tail-lashing angry. I ran at the door and thumped on it as loudly as I could. Again and again I did this, but still it did not open. Instead, the light came on where I was thundering, and Jenny came and picked me up. She was laughing, though I could not see what was funny at all. 'Oh Amber,' she said, 'I'm sorry, you can't go in there tonight, why not come in with us instead?'

Now, the door to the big bedroom is always left open, so any cat can come or go at any time of the day or night, but this time Jenny closed the door behind us (so I could not get out again) before she took me on the bed with her, where she stroked and stroked me so that I felt important and loved. This made me feel better, but I thought I should not appear too pleased, so I soon went off to the cave and slept well until there was scratching on the bedroom door. Silvester had, of course, been round-eyed surprised to find it shut. I heard Jenny get out of bed to let him in, but then she closed it once more and we all went to sleep till morning.

The visitors were kind to me when I saw them next day, and apologised for shutting me out, but they said the man could not have slept if I had stayed in the room with them, for he would have sneezed and sneezed, which would have kept me awake too, so we'd all had a better night the way things were. However, all the time he was talking so nicely I could sense he was stiff just being near me. Anyway, the visitors said goodbye later that day, and I was purring glad to have my room to myself again.

What a lot there is to understand about people isn't there, Dear Mary?

Puzzled purrs and love,

from Amber

Dear Dear Mary,

Purringly good news about the warming heart! As you know it's not been pleasant sleeping in the basket on top of it, nor in any other box or basket in its room, because it's so biting cold in there. Jenny grew tired of the clothes not drying, and we all thought it was more freezing in the warming heart room than outdoors, perhaps because all the blasting cold winds seemed to yowl through the way-in-way-out hole and gather near the basket. Before, when it was cosily warm, it felt good to have fresh, clean air from the garden, but now the menacing winter seemed to fill the room. We were all growling about it — to ourselves, to each other and also to Jenny.

Fortunately, the man came back a few days ago and banged about a lot in the warming heart room. Some people are cunningly clever aren't they Dear Mary? This one fixed a metal warmer to the wall, right next to the warming heart itself. There are many of these warmers on walls round the house, at least one in each room. In fact, I like to sit on the two wide ones in the kitchen, especially if they have clean clothes folded over them.

Anyway, I thought it was funny that this new warming heart couldn't warm its own room, but had to have a warmer on the wall to do it. Oh, but it does make it purring cosy. It's even better than before I think, so we all queue up to use the basket again and I'm happy to share it with Silvester, where we curve dreamily together. If Lion gets there first I pretend I'm not interested, and there's another comfy basket not far away, which I can make my bed, and this one's claw-stretchingly suitable too. Soon I hope the weather will turn warmer so that I can practise going further afield again.

By the way, now the warming heart room is cosy, I have let Jenny shut the door on my room as I do not feel I need to go in there any more. I have many special places to go, like the room where 'You Go' sleeps, Jenny and Darling's bedroom (the big bedroom) and the cave. I am also becoming braver again — at least indoors.

Warming purrs,

love Amber

Dear Dear Mary,

The weather is warmer at last, and I'm enjoying the garden, but I won't go far. I don't think I shall ever cross the bumpy road again because of the Terrible Thing. However, our garden is big enough, with the important tree and my wall for sunbathing, both of them near the way-in-way-out hole. I do not use the garden camp much now as it's darkly hidden and the sun can't find me. As you know I do love to relax in its bright warmth. There's also plenty for me to do in the garden without the need to travel further. I like it best when Jenny or the young men are working there. I wonder how they used to manage before I was here to help, for they seem to need me and say I give the best help they've ever had from any cat. But then, I had so much practice with you and Dear Albert didn't I?

It was just as well I had decided for myself that I didn't need my room any more, for there has been a stranger in it. He arrived suddenly in that basket with a lid and Jenny shut him in my room without even asking if I minded. She spent a lot of time with him, and the Gentle Mother came to visit him, and there were cooing voices behind the door. Silvester and I wondered if Stranger had come to live with us. After all, each of us had begun our lives in this house in my room and Jenny was making a big fuss of Stranger. I asked to see him and Jenny carried me into the room in her arms. Stranger was a big kitten, probably as old as I was when the Singing Person found me. Black and fluffy, he chirruped when he saw me, not finding me in the least frightening as he claw-stretched into the old bed cover and purred. I only peeped at him, swishing my tail cautiously, for he seemed full of confidence and I thought that if he burst out into the house he might be wildly-lively and grow bigger than Lion.

Honestly Dear Mary, I didn't know what to think, for Stranger had been lost and he needed a kindly home. I know what that is like, but this is my home now and I'm getting used to it the way it is. It makes me anxious to think that another cat could come and change things by being big and pouncing-powerful. He'd want his share of Jenny and the warming heart basket too. Silvester is not so young either and it might upset him as well, although probably not as much as me, because he's always so cheerful.

So I worried Dear Mary, but I need not have done. After a few days, Jenny put Stranger back in the basket with the lid, took him off in her moving room and we never saw him again. I felt sorry for him because Jenny was gone for many hours, so he must have had a lengthy journey, which will have been horrible for him.

At last, Jenny came back with the basket empty and, smiling, she said that Chester (he had a proper name now) had gone to live with her sister and a sad cat who'd lost his brother in an even Worse Thing than had happened to me. Silvester and I agreed that this story sounded rather the same as the one about Moses and Aaron. My guess is that Stranger (or Chester) is a cheery chirrupy chap like Silvester and I believe he will help the sad cat and the sad sister feel better. The comfort a cat can give is one of the best helps in the world for anyone who is sad, so he has an important job to do. He may have been sent specially, though I'm not sure who by, but that is an answer that I think you may know, Dear Mary.

Comforting purrs,

love Amber

Moses — Aaron's heart-to-heart friend

Dear Dear Mary,

I still do not know if it was a dream. The weather has become warmer and I am enjoying the garden again. So long as I do not go near the bumpy road I don't go trembly when I'm outside now. I've built a rubbing close relationship with Silvester and learnt to live with Lion and he with me — more or less. I now know that this is my home, for as I scrabble I sense that my paws belong in the earth here. I'm certain of all my territories and my work, which is to welcome and help — to help Jenny by purring encouragement whatever she's doing, the young men by following them round in the garden and 'You Go' by making sure he's not lonely in bed.

This particular day was sunny and Jenny had gone out, as she does (far too often). I was dozing on my wall when I heard the car return and then Jenny's voice calling me. I didn't hurry for I'm not a dog, but strolled round to the garden seat under the kitchen window. And there was a person, a gentle quiet person and the most surprising one I could ever have hoped to see. I could not rush to rub round you and purr on your lap for I could not believe it was really you, after all this lengthy-long time and all the missing of you. It felt so strange, so strange, yet purringly wonderful. I could sense it was you, from the tips of my whisker-twitching, through all of my heart-beating to the end wave of my tail and the stretch of my claw pads. It was a happiness too deep to show, lest it spoil and you would go, vanishing as suddenly as you had appeared.

We were all in the garden for many minutes and you kept saying, 'Oh Amber, Amber', and 'What a lovely home you have here'. And I purred and purred and thought, 'Well, yes, it's not so bad, though now I remember it again, nowhere could be as good as our life together.' And then you had to go, back to your safe new home. I could see that you were walking carefully, with your stick to help you, and with Jenny on your other side to make sure you were safe. You stroked and stroked me before you went and we were both glad and sad at the same moment.

Then you were gone, but the sun still shone and the seat still warmed me where you'd sat. So I stayed there thinking of you, knowing that you love me and feeling the comforting warmth of that knowing, like sunshine inside me.

I think I must have fallen into what is called a reverie, for suddenly Jenny was beside me again, saying softly, 'Oh Amber, you're still here on the seat'. And I knew that she loved me too for, as we felt each other's sunshine, she stroked me gently and all seemed well — all seemed very well, my very dear, Dear Mary.

Purring dreamily,

with my love,

Amber

Dear Dear Mary,

The summer months have passed peacefully since my wonderful dream of you. Lion and I have more of an understanding and Silvester is a good friend. One item of news is that I am glad to have another way-in-and-out which is more or less all mine as the others don't seem to use it. There's a window in the kitchen with a seat under it, which is purring comfortable as it has a cushion on it. Jenny likes to leave this window open as soon as the weather is pleasant and, from the sill, I can step either onto the rail that guards the stone steps that lead to the back door, or onto the stone shelf beneath the window, and so make my way into the garden. Then, when I'm ready I make my way back in again. Of course it only works properly when the window's open and sometimes I have to sit outside on the sill and wait for a person to oblige, which is fleasomely irritating.

'You Go' does not live in his room now, but comes in his moving room to see us, which pleases us all, especially Rosie as he takes her for walks in it sometimes, while Lion purrs thunderously to see him and rolls around pretending he's a mardy cat.

Jenny has just been away for more than a few days, which is thoughtless of her, as it's the second time she and Darling have done this since I saw you. However, you must not worry, Dear Mary, as there are some new people who look after us. They live here all the time when Jenny's away and sleep in my room. They are called Pippa and Ray and are kindly, which is good because Silvester has not been quite himself recently. I do not know exactly what is different, for he's still cheerful, but he seems to be walking restlessly about. There is something ...

Purrs of love,

from Amber

Dear Dear Mary,

Much has happened to tell you, mostly about Silvester who is now famous. Only a day or two after Jenny came home with Darling we had some visitors. A woman asked Jenny lots of questions and wrote down what she answered, and a man said he was making pictures with one of those black boxes. It was to do with the book that Jenny has been writing about all her cats, all her cats except me, but she says she has an idea for me to have my own book one day. Since I am so clever at writing letters I should like that.

Anyway, the person who was asking the questions stayed for a long time and I welcomed them both in my polite hostess way, so that they thought

I was perfect, even though it was Silvester they had mainly come to see. Of course, Lion did not call by to greet the visitors. He would think he was too busy, which I thought was a sorrowing pity, for I was proud to be Silvester's friend and to see that they thought he was a somewhat special cat. He walked into the room to talk to them without Jenny calling him, as I did too, and he stayed hunting-still in her arms to have his picture made using the black box. ('Hunting-still' is funny now I think about it, because he has never caught anything in his whole life!)

The people were purring pleased with their visit. They make the newspaper which we use to dry our feet when we come in through the way-in-way-out hole. Darling also has heaps of it each day and it's warmly comfortable to sit on. I do not exactly understand how a picture of Silvester will help make a newspaper, but it will somehow make him even more famous. There is also a picture of him on the cover of the book, which makes him look extremely important.

But oh, Dear Mary, you will remember that I said Silvester has not been quite himself. Well, Jenny noticed it too, and when she came home she gave him some of the medicine that he took some months ago when he was not so well and it made him better. This time it can't have worked, for one morning soon afterwards, when I was in the cave, I heard Jenny say to Darling when they woke up, 'Silvester's not on the bed'. For he was always there, snuggling up to Jenny and drinking water from the glass she kept alongside her own, especially for him. She was twitching worried and went straightaway to look for him, and I went too.

We couldn't find him in the kitchen, nor in the warming heart room, nor anywhere downstairs. So next we went out into the garden, with Jenny calling all the time. We soon found him standing in the flowerbed near my wall — just standing as if he didn't know how to move, the poor, dear chap. I wondered how long he'd been there like that. It must have been so frightening for him. He chirruped loudly when Jenny picked him up and purred and purred as she cuddled him, but she and I knew that something had gone very wrong. We took him inside and Jenny put him gently on the worktop near the way-in-way-out hole, and stood back from him for a moment, while talking to him all the time. At once it became clear to Jenny and me that Silvester couldn't see. He was blind as a shut-eye. How yowling dreadful for him, but he was so pleased to be with us and said he felt safe now Jenny was there, because she's always known what to do.

Jenny took Silvester in her moving room to see the Clever Vet, who apparently said he had had a stroke, which I didn't understand, for being stroked makes a cat feel safe and purry. Anyway, he could not remember anyone stroking him, just being unable to settle and needing the air of the garden, then a sort of sleep pouncing on him suddenly with no waking from darkness, which frightened him. He could not tell where he was and could not seem to move, so he purred with relief when he heard Jenny looking for him.

Straightaway I made the decision that, as Silvester had been kind to me when I needed a friend, so now I would try to do the same for him and help him find his way if I could. Fortunately, Jenny knows a lot of useful men and, later that morning, two of her special friends came to look at the warming heart room to see what they could do to help, for Silvester couldn't use the steps up to the way-in-way-out hole any more.

They made a marvellous path of wood, with small pieces across it for his paws to grip, so he would not slip. The marvellous path led up from the floor to a small platform right next to the warming heart. It made a bridge between the worktop route to the way-in-way-out hole and the basket on top of the warming heart. I thought it was a claw-stretchingly good idea, and started going up it myself straightaway, for the wooden steps I'd always enjoyed using were now covered up by the marvellous path.

As each day went by Silvester got better and better at finding his way round the house. He has always had huge long whiskers and now he used them to touch and feel every space and doorway. Jenny had put a tray for him on the floor near the marvellous path, but he soon found his way up the path, outside, and down the length of wall onto the steady pile of logs that takes him safely down into the garden. Jenny has been kindly, caressing him and taking a lot of trouble to make sure he keeps safe. I've been out in the garden with him trying to guide him around until he learns it by his whiskers, which he is doing quickly.

One day I was in the cave and, to my surprise, I found Silvester climbing up to the top shelf beside me. He is amazing isn't he? I was worried about how he would get down again, but he chirruped cheerfully, 'Not to worry' and, sure enough, later on when he was ready to leave, he stepped out of the cupboard and onto the towels on the rail. Then he slid down the towels to the floor, much more quietly than in his old way of thumping down. Jenny could not believe he was still going in and out of the cupboard until she saw him do it with her own eyes. Of course, he easily finds his way onto the bed again by climbing up the bedspreading cloth and spends all night on Jenny's chest or on her head, where he feels safe. He can even find his glass of water and drink from it again. In the kitchen he still manages to get onto the worktop near the kettle, by climbing patiently from the seat under the window. He's wonderful at finding new ways of doing things, though he did paddle in the sugar bowl one day.

Silvester has told me that he's feeling much better again, for the Clever Vet has given Jenny pills to give him, which help his heart to beat in a steady rhythm. It was running too quickly before. He says it felt as if it was rushing away from him, which made him go walking and walking trying to catch it up. He's becoming more and more his old self, just going a little slower now he's using his whiskers and ears to see. I must say he's grateful and uncomplaining about taking his pills. He never ever

spits them out like I did, for he says Jenny has always done right by him and he knows she's trying her best now. I suppose the main thing for a cat is to feel safe, which Silvester does, so long as Jenny is there.

I've not mentioned Lion in all this. As you know he puts himself first, but he's always been purring friendly with Rosie and Silvester. He remembers how kind Silvester was to him when he arrived as a small kitten with huge ears. I suppose he's thought of Silvester as a big brother and it's hard to see someone you thought was strong become weak. He did not try to help like I did when Silvester suddenly could not see. I think he turned a blind eye to what was happening, but he was not unkind. Then yesterday, when I went up to the cave, Silvester was already in there and Lion was cuddled up close beside him. So I crept away and went down to the basket on the warming heart, feeling glad that Lion was care-loving Silvester too. He needs all the comfort we can give him.

Loving purrs, concernedly, from Amber

1998

Dear Dear Mary,

How are you? I can hardly believe it's more than a year since I wrote to you, but I've been very busy looking after Silvester. I've also caught a few shrews as presents for Jenny, to help cheer her up as I know she worries about him. Even Lion has tried to do his part, bringing her two small rabbits.

Jenny told me back in the summer that I've been living with her for two whole years, which she says has gone quickly, but it seems a long time to me. Anyway, the day she said it, the door to my room happened to be open so I went and had a contented roll on the bed, partly to show that I feel more at home here now and partly to remember you, Dear Mary, and our purring time together. I think I told you that 'You Go' doesn't live here now. He comes to see us though, with his lovely Jo who likes cats.

I was always pleased to see them, but now they have a Cowley dog who is huge. He must be called Cowley because it is just like having a cow in the house when he comes, though he is much more bouncy than a cow and doesn't eat grass. Poor Rosie hates him as he won't leave her alone, even when she curls her lip snarlingly at him. So now she hides upstairs whenever she hears him arrive. The great Cowley dog enjoys playing in Jenny's garden and it's easy for Lion and I to keep out of his way. Of course Jenny takes special care that Silvester is safe when he comes, though, to be fair to him, he doesn't take much notice of cats as he's got two of his own called Pudding and Pie who show him who's boss.

With Silvester it's been a year of ups and downs, though it's now become roundly-rounds as I'll tell you. His eyes are not changing any more since he went blind. As with all cats, they used to change, moon-like, depending on whether it was light or dark, from a shape like a claw in the sky to a circle as round as a feeding dish. Now his eyes are always round like full milky moons. He has to have pills every day and, though Jenny has been away sometimes, Pippa and Ray have always come to live with us to make sure he is safe, though he does seem to grow frailer as the weeks go by. This has never stopped him being cheerful, however, and able to find his way everywhere, so that no-one would know he is doing it blindly. But then a few weeks ago it all changed again.

Jenny found him missing from the bed when she woke up, and there was Silvester going round and round in circles on the lawn in the front garden. He could no longer find his way and Jenny had to rescue him. The Clever Vet said that he'd had another accident to his brain, that people call a stroke, though I still think it's a strange name for it. Since this has happened Silvester finds his way by going round and round, until he's able to break the circle and go to the doorway, or the bed, or wherever. However, I was worried when I saw him trying to go out of the way-in-way-out hole. What would happen if he fell off the wall? I went to tell Jenny and she came quickly, carried him gently into the garden and watched over him.

We are slowly finding a pattern but it's different now. Jenny takes Silvester into the garden every few hours and lets him have a peaceful time out there. He can still get onto the bed by climbing up the covers, and he then sleeps on Jenny and drinks from his glass of water. He's always cheerful too, never growing impatient with the circling, circling, till he finds the way. A few days ago he even climbed up into the cave and slid back down the towels as he used to do.

He enjoys his food and the basket on the warming heart, where I cuddle up to him and wash his ears. He purrs contentedly at level ten when I do that and it makes me purring happy to help him in this way. But I know Silvester is an old cat now and will always need a lot of help to live cheerfully, which he does. He never ever complains and everybody loves him. Jenny doesn't even go out for the day without some caring person coming to see to him, take him into the garden and give him his afternoon pill. We're all getting used to watching over him, even Lion is kindly.

Protectively purring,

love Amber

1999

Dear Dear Mary,

Earlier this year I was not purring well myself. I was having to eat grass to make myself be sick, but even after doing that I still could not fancy much food, though I was still lively in other ways. I expect you will remember that when I came to live with Jenny I had a round tummy. Well I've lost it. I don't know where a heavy little tummy can go, but it's gone, and I went so thin that Jenny was worried about me. I was worried about me too. Jenny took me to see the Clever Vet twice, and the second time, after not giving me any breakfast she left me there with the kindly nurse. I hate being away from home, it's yowling upsetting and this was for many hours I think, though I was asleep for some of the time, after the Clever Vet had stuck a needle into me.

When I woke up my mouth felt different and a tooth was missing, a tooth that hadn't exactly hurt me but was uncomfortable in my mouth. So that was good and when Jenny came to take me home that was better still. The only nuisance was that for many days she opened my mouth and put small pills down my throat, unless I spat them out secretly, but she watched me until she was sure they'd gone. The Clever Vet was pleased with me when Jenny took me back to see him. I'd stopped being sick, was enjoying my food again and had put on some weight, though the round tummy hasn't come back.

How are you now Dear Mary? Of course, one of the reasons that I came to live here was that you, like Silvester, could not see to be safe on your own. He's going round and round more and more, trying to find his way. I hope you don't have to go round to find your way, for I think it must make you weak and tired. But Silvester never complains. He's still cheerful. He looks older and more wobbly as time goes by and needs us all to watch over him. Jenny spends a lot of time looking after him. He eats well but is thin, but then he never did have a tummy like me. Some cats never do, do they?

Our other news this year is that Big Harry has come to live here again sometimes. When he does, he's in the room which used to belong to 'You Go'. I'm glad as it gives me someone else to visit and purr on. It's also another person to help us care for Silvester.

Watchfully purring, love Amber

Dear Dear Mary,

I am tremblingly sad to tell you that Silvester died yesterday, but it was purring peaceful and he's still with us, but lying under some flowers in the garden.

He had been growing weaker as the days passed, but was always cheerful, spending every night purring on Jenny in bed, with Lion often on the end

near Darling's feet and me in the cave. The house had grown sparkly for Christmas and we all thought Silvester would be with us to enjoy it, but then something killingly happened to him. Jenny and Darling were away for just one night and everything was as usual, with Pippa and Ray looking after us, sleeping in the sharing-bed so that Silvester would have company. And he was all right until the middle of the morning. Then a huge accident must have pounced on his brain and knocked his head on one side so that he could hardly walk, and Pippa and Ray were so kindly and worried, and spoke to Jenny, who must have been coming home anyway, for she was soon there and Silvester was flopped in the basket on the warming heart, where Pippa and Ray had put him. He was still purring cheerfully, for I suppose he felt safe there, but there was no room for me without squashing him.

When Jenny got home she found Silvester could still eat and his tummy was still working in the garden, but she stayed close by him all the time. The way his poor head was most comfortable was either resting in the basket on the warming heart or, better still, purring on Jenny's chest while she lay with him on the sofa and then in bed. Jenny and Darling were sad, for we all knew that not even the Clever Vet could make Silvester better this time. Lion was on the sharing-bed all night too for, being a cat, he was not, of course, insensitive to what was happening to his friend. In the morning Jenny must have left the main door open so that people could come in, for she was on the bed cuddling Silvester (with me in the cave) for a lengthy time, when suddenly the Clever Vet and the kindly nurse were there, and I heard Jenny say, 'He's still purring'.

It was quiet then. Jenny was crying and it was as if Silvester was asleep. Even then I could almost feel he was still purring. She brought Lion to say goodbye but he took it hard and went off quickly. Jenny wrapped Silvester up beautifully and I stayed with her all the time she was putting him to rest in the garden. Jenny needed me to help her, for she was weeping, weeping, but it was all so peaceful and Silvester had even died cheerful. I wish all cats could have such a good life. He was a true friend and I'll never forget him — dear old Silvester.

Purring with fond memories,

love Amber

2000

The loss of Silvester cast a little sadness over Christmas, as I had somehow expected that he would have spent just one more with us. On the other hand I was so grateful that the end had come when I could be with him, and no cat could have had a happier life. Now it was time to look forward. It was after all a new millennium and the long awaited opportunity to have two kittens.

Unlike dogs who breed all the year round, cats tend not to breed in the winter, so our local animal sanctuary, 'Windyway', did not have any kittens, but made a note of my request. I was lucky. A week later, in early February, I had a call to say that over in Crewe, Fudge had abandoned an unsatisfactory home and moved a few doors away, announcing that she would like to live with Pete and Teresa, then presenting them with four kittens as a thank you gift. They had rung 'Windyway' on the recommendation of the RSPCA to say that they needed homes for two of them. Not for long they didn't!

The next day saw me take my mother to meet our prospective new babies. She was growing frailer herself so outings had to be chosen carefully, but this was one not to be missed. Fudge was an elegant, semi-long-haired, black, ginger-and-white cat with an affectionate disposition. The two kittens that were spoken for were like her. The other two were a ginger-and-white male and an all black female. They were fluffy like their mum, totally adorable as kittens and promising to grow into beautiful cats. Our very first cat, Sam, had looked just like this little girl, so I was particularly thrilled. I arranged to pick them up a week later when they would be mature enough to leave their mother.

We had fun over the next day or two trying to decide on names, and then they just seemed to choose themselves. These were, after all, millennium kittens so what better names could there be than Mille and Lenni? There was only one possible snag, some of us may remember a television ventriloquist's dummy called Lenny the Lion. We would have to avoid calling him that or it would confuse Amber!

Many years ago when we were installing two kittens (Moses and Aaron) one of them vanished, causing panic until found in an impossibly tiny space behind the work surfaces in the kitchen. I was to remember this the day Mille and Lenni arrived when, having left them for a few minutes in their nursery (Amber's special room) while I went to feed and exercise Rosie, I returned to find not a 50% but a 100% loss. No kittens! Fruitless and ever more frantic searching began convincing me that someone must have climbed in through the shut window and stolen them. However, Amber came to the rescue and, the crisis behind us, Mille and Lenni could not have been easier, healthier or more rewarding kittens, though Amber, ever sensitive, took time to adjust to the newcomers.

The year 2000 was busy, not only with the joys of two maturing kittens, but with preparations for Hugo's wedding to Jo in September. The ceremony was to take place at Gawsworth Hall, but the reception-come-party would be in a marquee in our garden. When the marquee arrived Mille decided it was hers for dancing in — though not while full of wedding guests. It was Amber who was entranced then, having all these people to entertain. She helped to look after the Bandit Beatles while they had their meal in the kitchen, then played the perfect hostess to anyone coming into the house seeking a quieter moment during the evening.

In 1998 we had bought a holiday cottage in Cumbria and, by the winter of 1999, all the renovation work had been completed. Thus it was that Mille and Lenni, too small to be left on their own, accompanied us up to Greengarth along with Rosie. They had a wonderful time in this safe haven for two small cats, particularly enjoying the dark of the old barn which will one day become an annexe to the cottage. We took them three times and, on each occasion they grew more venturesome, so that by the third visit they were starting to travel next door in order to catch mice and shrews. We worried about the birds and the precious red squirrel, who did not seem to be cat aware, since few local people have cats.

Having decided that it would have to be the kittens' last trip to Greengarth we missed their cheery company and this gave birth to another idea. I'd sometimes worried that Amber could never be as happy with us as she had been with Mary, being the only animal with no competition from other cats, and certainly unthreatened by the likes of Bernard. Why not try to give her a taste of this to enjoy again by taking her to Greengarth with us? True she would have to endure the two hour journey, but once there I had a hunch it could be just what she needed. We therefore planned to start taking her with us in the spring of 2001 until the gruesome Foot and Mouth epidemic intervened. The cottage being on National Trust sheep country, it was difficult even for us to go, as it involved lugging our baggage through the farm gate onto the fell, first dipping our feet in the astringent solution that haunted our wellies for the duration of our stay and beyond. We could not take Rosie, never mind try introducing a cat.

Thus it was not until December 2001 that Amber could come with us. We had celebrated the arrival of the new millennium at Greengarth and it had since become a tradition to spend New Year's Eve in Cumbria — a tradition of which Amber heartily approved when she finally joined us, for it gave her a happiness and confidence which she took back with her to Throstles' Nest, where she had the joy and satisfaction of relating her news to Mary.

Dear Dear Mary,

Lion and I have missed Silvester sadly. It has not exactly brought us closer together but the empty space is something we share; we are on either side of it, with understanding like a joining place between us. The Christmas sparkle was not so noticeable this year but I made a special fuss of Jenny because she needed me and I think Lion did the same.

Then yesterday, Jenny came in very quietly but talking all the time to that basket, the one which always means travelling about for one of us. She went straight up to my room, stayed there for only a few minutes and then came down and made a big fuss of me and Lion, who happened to be inside as well. She gave us our food and stroked us more than usual. Lion and I exchanged looks, which we never used to do unless we had to. We thought it was suspicious. While Jenny took Rosie in the garden to practise killing sticks Lion went upstairs. I decided to bide my time.

When Jenny came back she went straight up again and wouldn't let Lion go into my room — quite right, of course. He came grumping down and hurled himself out into the garden, muttering, 'Creatures', as he went, 'Little creatures'. I went upstairs on my quiet paws to see Jenny coming out of my room looking trembling upset. She then searched round the house several times before going back in there. I could hear her calling, 'Kitty, kitty kitties, oh, wherever are you?' I just sat there on the landing, thinking, 'I know those little creatures are in that room, whoever they are, but why ever is Jenny so worried, and why does she want them anyway, when she's got me who is so lovely and gentle?'

But I never like to see Jenny upset so I just waited and waited in my patient way. I could hear her moving the present boxes out from under the bed, and opening the cupboard door, and doing it all lots of times. From under the door I could feel her worry scuttering round the room like a desperate mouse. At last she came out again looking more anxious than ever, so I gave her a kindly chirrup and offered to help.

Jenny said, 'Oh yes Amber, you come in and tell me if they're all right'. So I walked in carefully and looked at their food bowls, but I didn't think much of what she was giving them. Then I looked over my shoulder at Jenny, a look that said, 'Well, they're in here all right, I can feel them, the strange little creatures, they're tucked away safely, no need to worry'. Jenny understands me quite well these days. She picked me up, cuddled me and said, 'Oh thank you Amber, I'll keep looking'. So I left her to it, though of course I could have shown her exactly where they were, hiding in that tiny box with a hole in it in the corner. I could have shown her, but I think that would have been going a bit far, don't you Dear Mary? Then, as I went downstairs to see how Lion was getting on, I heard Jenny say, 'Oh there you are, fancy you getting in there'.

Sometimes she's sensible, so she didn't try to make them come out, just left them till morning. Mind you, she slept in there, on my bed, all night. Darling had to sleep on his own.

I don't think I'm pleased to have little creatures in the house Dear Mary. I'd just got my life the way I liked it, keeping people company in any room I wished, with a goodly working arrangement with Lion about which bits of the house are his and which are mine. I was also getting more turns in the warming heart basket now dear old Silvester doesn't need it any more. I've not seen them yet so I don't know what the little creatures are like but I'm hoping that, like Stranger, they'll only stay for a few days.

Wishfully purring,

love Amber

Dear Dear Mary,

Well, so much for hoping ... the little creatures are staying. They've got names — Mille and Lenni. They're brother and sister, and have fluffy coats, not smoothly beautiful like mine. Little Lenni's is golden, which is my favourite colour for a cat, and Mille is black all over.

I say they are cats, but only just. They are very little. Jenny carried them down, both together, to show them to me when I was sitting on my cushion in the kitchen. They seemed very interested to see me but I didn't give them much encouragement. I mean, I don't wish them any harm but I don't see why they have to be here at all. For once, Lion and I agree.

Fortunately, Jenny keeps them shut up in one room so they aren't a great nuisance to me, except that I would prefer it if they weren't in my room. One pleasure is, that when Jenny sees me she makes an extra fuss of me. Mind you, she should do really, with all the visitors the little creatures are getting. People keep coming by like a pageant, in the front door, up the stairs, into my room, shut the door, cooey cooey attention. I don't remember such a fuss when I first moved here, do you, Dear Mary?

All my loving purrs,

Amber

Dear Dear Mary,

The latest news is that Jenny has let the little creatures come out of what used to be my room and is letting them go into the big bedroom. So now they sleep in there together with Jenny and Darling. Rosie is sometimes in there too but the door is kept shut, which it never used to be. This means Lion can't go in, which makes him grouchy, for he used to sleep on the sharing bed if he felt like it (more often now Silvester is not here any more) and I would sleep in the cave, coming out to say 'Hello' after Lion had gone to get on with his early morning activities.

The little creatures can't get into the cave (which joins up Jenny and Darling's bedroom with the place with the white bath in it) because Jenny keeps the door on their side shut, but somehow I don't feel so keen about going upstairs now the little creatures are up there, so I miss the cave and going in Jenny's study, and oh, all sorts of places. It's also nastily cold and wet outside, so I can't go and enjoy any of my walls, or walks, or camps in the garden. Fortunately, the radiators are cosy-warm in the kitchen, and Lion and I take turns in the warming heart basket on the clean washing, but I'm not as pleased as I was before *they* came.

I hope I can give you cheerier news next time.

Purring hopefully,

with love,

Amber

Dear Dear Mary,

As you know I've been feeling rather unsettled having these little creatures living with us and this hasn't been helped by the cold weather. However, they do not seem in any way dangerous and, because she must be feeling guilty about bringing them here without asking me or Lion, Jenny has been especially kind. Then yesterday it turned warmer and today it was lovely and sunny.

I was enjoying being in the garden, when suddenly out of the house the little Lenni creature came running. He's not very graceful, but merrily he came up to the stone table where I was sitting and looked at me politely. I thought, well, perhaps he's not so bad, so I just leant down and gave him a gentle pat, and he chirruped up at me, then went skippety skippety off towards the gate in my wall. Jenny was watching him, while the little Mille creature was creeping along the top of the back door steps before coming down them and walking up to me. (I was on the ground by this time.) I'm quite pleased that she isn't a boy, so I gave her an even gentler pat and then she chirruped off behind the flower pots and bins. Both the little creatures seem to think the garden is beautiful and exciting, and I'm glad because I may be able to teach them some things about it.

Then of course Lion had to appear. What a show off! First he spat at little Lenni when he went up to say 'Hello', then he rushed up the wall, onto the trellis and swung around on top of the arch where the climbing plant trails about. Jenny was laughing and saying he was clever. Well, he is quick and agile, but he was enough to depress a kitten, or me, as next he rushed down off the arch, flew past little Lenni, who'd just gone through it, and was suddenly up the old tree, sitting in the fork and showing us all how skilful he is. Little Lenni couldn't take his eyes off him. I expect he wondered how he got up there, so high, so quickly. I gave up watching then and went back to the stone table under the kitchen window.

Jenny doesn't leave little Lenni and Mille on their own outside. She watches them all the time and calls them — like she used to do with me when I first came to live here and was wondering whether to stay or try to find you. I don't think the kittens will try to return to wherever they came from. They seem to like it here and maybe, being still so small, they can't really remember their other place. I don't mind them so much now.

More cheerful purrs, love Amber

Dear Dear Mary,

What do you think, Jenny has gone off with Rosie and taken little Lenni and Mille with her. I feel quite sorry for them as she's taken them in her horrible moving room which, as you know, I sometimes call a tin can because it's so noisy. Rather them than me, and it gives me some peace in the house, for it's gone nastily biting cold. I hope you're staying indoors Dear Mary, for I'm going outside hardly at all.

I've been keeping Big Harry (who stays here sometimes) company in his bedroom. He seems to like that. We were having a purring relaxing time together until Guess Who? appeared. P'raps he was bored, as it was so cold outside, but really, does he have to be so aggressively unpleasant? He growled and pounced on me. Of course, I swore back at him, but he is so strong. Anyway, Big Harry picked him up and dropped him over the bannister onto the stairs, which served him right, even though it's only a little leap for Lion, who can nearly fly. But it must have made him feel a bit silly, while I felt smug and made more of a fuss than ever of Big Harry, who shut the door, so Lion couldn't be up to his tricks again.

I don't understand why Jenny doesn't want to be here all the time with me, do you Dear Mary? But I suppose I am getting used to her funny ways. She always comes back again at last, and the food never stops, so it's not so bad, except I do wish the cold biting wind would go away, so I could get on with being in the garden.

Purring wistfully,

love Amber

Dear Dear Mary,

Well she's back and so is Rosie and so are little Lenni and Mille. I surprise myself; I find I'm rather pleased to see them, after all they do admire me and realise that I'm a special senior cat, which is more than can be said for someone else!

Little Lenni had us all rather worried soon after he came home. First Jenny couldn't find him at bedtime, though she knew he had to be in the house. (I'll come back to that later.) She hunted in all the usual places like the cave, no little Lenni. Then she hunted everywhere else, but still no little Lenni. Then we heard all this frightened squeaky miaowing coming from Big Harry's room, and there on the bed was this lump under the cover going round and round, and up and down, squeaking and squeaking. It was a Lenni lump. He'd got inside the cover of the duvet and couldn't get out. I think he's a bit too venturesome.

Both little Mille and little Lenni love the garden, like me, but I'm afraid Lenni is too easily impressed by Lion. The other day he got on top of the arch, just like Lion does, and then, would you believe it, today he climbed high into the ancient tree where there's a nest made of a twisty plant, which smells lovely when it flowers. He sat up there for ages, so we could all see how cleverly he'd climbed. He was so pleased I couldn't be cross,

especially as he's so polite when we meet, but frankly, I'm not sure that it's wise at his age. I mean he could have got stuck, couldn't he?

As I said, Jenny does not let little Mille and Lenni go outside just when they want; she keeps a close watch on them. This has made arrangements for me and Lion slightly less convenient. The marvellous path that was in the warming heart room for Silvester to clamber up gingerly to reach the outdoors has been taken away. I used to find that path useful too, so I rather miss it. Also, the door to the warming heart room is often shut, which would be all right if the cat flap in it was still tied up open as it used to be. However, it's now closed, for little Mille and Lenni can't push strongly enough to open it to go through. Of course, I am strong and clever enough, but I don't like the bother of it. I do understand though, how important it is to keep the kittens safe.

I've been surprised at the interest they're causing. Jenny's friends still go cooey when they see them. By the way, little Lenni has an unreasonably long tail, which goes dippy at the end. Little Mille has a sensible tail like mine (though fluffier) which she holds prettily upwards as she chirrup-trots around.

Cheery purrs,

love Amber

Dear Dear Mary,

I've some sort-of friends I quite like. They live in the house across the bumpy road. They are all the same beautiful colour as me and little Lenni, which is sometimes called 'ginger', but 'golden' is much better, isn't it? There are two of them with strange names — Grubby and Filth — though they are as clean as me, and then another one arrived, who is completely golden, with no white fur at all. He was always bigger than our little creatures and is still finding his way around his own plot without coming on our drive. But Grubby and I, or Filth and I, sometimes sit side by side on one of our tin cans, or beside the garage, so they soon found out about little Mille and Lenni.

A few days ago, when they were out playing in the garden, Grubby came in our garden too while I was watching, and was following little Lenni around. He seemed to think he was all right. Then he watched little Mille do some dancing leaps after a fly. We both thought it was a graceful, amazing, high-on-air dance. I felt proud of her. Grubby must have told Filth because next day, much to my surprise, when I was sitting on my seat by the window, in he strolled. Big Harry was surprised too and told Jenny afterwards. I did not think it wise to tell Lion, who would have been very tail lashing about it. I thought Filth was very brave, but he seemed to think it was important for him to check out 'the new kits on our patch'.

One of the few good things about having Lion around is that he protects us all from Travelling Tom. He comes from far away but would like to own everything. He comes by at least once a week and I make sure I keep well out of his reach. He knew very quickly about little Mille and Lenni, long before they ever went outside into the garden, and he tried to come into the house one day but Lion stood bravely in the way-in-way-out hole and told him fiercely to get off our beat. I think he'll return though, especially now the kittens are going outside, so I keep a close watch on them, and so does Jenny, as we need to make sure they come to no harm.

They are very nesh as yet. Do you know that word Dear Mary? It means feeling cold or hurting easily and, of course, all kittens do. I remember when I was having my horrible time in the hedge, that I was all shivery and cold, and I was bigger than little Mille and Lenni are now.

Fortunately, they've learnt about the essentials of life very quickly, for example, they know how to run up the wall, in through the way-in-way-out hole, then through that flap in the door, which, I'm glad to say, is now tied-up-open again. So they can make themselves safe, or comfy, whenever they want.

On the whole they are also quite sensitive to my being more important than they are, but now and again they make a mistake, like the other day when little Mille came in from the cold outside, leapt onto the worktop in the warming heart room, saw my cosy box and hopped in, just as I came in behind her. I was going to be upset, but fortunately Jenny saw it all happen and lifted little Mille out and onto the floor, explaining to her that it was Amber's box and that Mille had plenty of other cosy and more hidey places she could go for a sleep. Mille then went off cheerily to find one of them and all was well.

Of course there is nothing quite like being the only cat in a home, but now I am getting more used to them I do not mind Mille and Lenni so much. I like Lenni because he is beautifully golden like me, and Mille because it is good to have another girl cat about the place. I wish Jenny would stop shutting the door to the big bedroom at night though.

Purring with love,

from Amber

Dear Dear Mary,

Little Mille and Lenni are not so little now, for they are half-a-year old and are nearly as big as me; in fact they look as if they are as big, but then a lot of it is fluff. The other day Jenny took them off in the basket in her moving room and they were gone for many hours. When she brought them back again they smelt of the Clever Vet and Mille had a bald patch on her side — not fluffy at all! She was quiet for a few hours but Lenni seemed just the same as usual, saying it had been rather boring but he'd had a good sleep. They were both purring and glad to be home, as cats always are.

You know I said I wished Jenny would stop shutting the door to the big bedroom, well my wish has come true. I was in the garden on the large patch of grass at the back the other evening talking to Rosie and Darling, when a flying Mille arrived beside us. We all saw her do it. One moment she was on the balcony watching us, the next she was flying. I was round-eyed impressed, not even Lion has ever flown from there, and she made it look easy. A day or two later I saw Lenni do the same thing. Copy cat. Anyway, now Jenny has solved the mystery of how Mille was suddenly out when she'd been shut in for the night. After that Jenny stopped

shutting the bedroom door. If Mille and Lenni can fly they can certainly take care of themselves.

Lion is pleased, saying it's not before time, and he's immediately started going to sleep on the sharing-bed some nights. Of course he expects Lenni to make way for him, but he doesn't go far, sleeping at Darling's feet. Lion, who is not gentle or subtle, and has to stomp his point, sleeps on top of Jenny, to prove he has the loudest purr in the house. Mille has seldom slept on the bed at night anyway, preferring the chair where Darling puts his clothes. She loves him purring much and says he has a soothing scent that makes her feel safe.

I don't think I ever explained that Mille and Lenni have their food on the window shelf in the big bedroom. It's different from ours because they're young, while Lion and I are of more middle years. It's only another kind of biscuit, so nothing to go wild about, but Lion thinks it's important to show that we have as much right to eat their food as they have to sneak some of ours from the warming heart room.

I hope you still enjoy mouse-tasty food where you live now Dear Mary and that the weather treats you more kindly. It keeps raining wetly here.

Damply purring,

love Amber

Dear Dear Mary,

We've had a wedding in the house. Well, it was in the house, the garden, up and down the bumpy road, nearly in the slope-side field — in fact in everywhere I call home. I've never seen Jenny run so fast as in those last few days before the Wedding Day. Faster and faster she went, twirling ribbons and bows and flowers, moving tables, shoving chairs, lighting sparkly Christmas lights, and finally bobbing about with beautiful blue-and-white balloons till everywhere felt happy. As you know, Dear Mary, cats do not like change of any sort, we like home to stay the same as we know it, so I was surprised at myself for enjoying it all so much.

The most extraordinary surprise was the huge cloth house that rose up whitely, built by some men in the garden. These were the first people who came to help with the Wedding Day, but then there were many others as time went by, some with many thick black wires for lights in the garden and in the cloth house, others building little white huts under the trees for what Jenny called 'convenience', the farmer discussing the wetness of the weather on his field, and so it went on until the day itself. I could not possibly have counted all the people with flowers, balloons, bottles, table-cloths, cooking pans, and so on, for there were far more than ten, probably ten again and again.

However, to go back to the huge cloth house (apparently called a marquee) which stood in the back garden into which Mille flies from the balcony. It was one enormous space with no cosy rooms inside, but it grew a soft carpet over the grass. Then came the tables and chairs. I didn't go inside but watched from the doorway. Mille thought Jenny had put the marquee there for her to dance in, for it was raining yowling wetly outside. She leapt and pranced all over the floor of it, while Lenni wafted about waving his longer than long feathery tail. There was no sign of Lion however. He was growly about his garden being taken over.

Meanwhile, one day I noticed Big Harry in the slope-side field and went to watch him from the garden hedge. He was solemnly moving what the cows had left behind. It took him hours and hours on two whole days working with a big shovel, for there are usually many cows in the field and, unlike cats, they are not tidy about that sort of thing. I was not sure why he was doing it until the Wedding Day itself, but then I could see that there were so many people that if any more had come we might have had to put them in the field for a while, though they would have needed rubbery feet, for it was so wet after the rain any moving room would have got muddied-in-stuck.

The day before the wedding Jenny's friend arrived all the way from somewhere called France. She was purry warm and had a different way of talking. Jenny laughed when her friend talked about 'The Weeding', which I thought was unkind for we all have our own way of saying things, just as good as any other. Myself I think words should be changed to suit how one feels at any one moment, whether talking or writing them down.

Anyway, the friend, whose name is Catherine, was a big help to Jenny, who ran around so fast on the day itself that I thought she might fly like Mille! Round and round, round and round, faster and faster, until suddenly there she was looking serene in a long frock, as if she'd been quiet all morning, and it did go quiet for a lengthy time after that, as all the family went off in their moving rooms and it was only the people in Mille's marquee who were bustling busily. It stopped raining on the day and the sun came out, as if it was as glad as I was to see 'You Go' looking so happy and Jo (who I like a lot) so smilingly beautiful in her delicately frothy, trailing white dress. I'd never seen anyone look so glowing.

As many people started to arrive inside the house, two were already sitting in a corner playing soft music, a gentle young woman blowing on a slender silvery pipe (not curvy like a saxyphone) and a young man squeezing a big box in and out. It made everyone feel soothed and happier than ever. Then more and more people arrived so that I could see why we might have needed some of them to go into the slope-side field, except that they slowly moved on into Mille's marquee, where they did a lot of talking and eating. There was talking and eating in the kitchen too, for several young men came in there to have their supper and I made them as purringly welcome as only I can. Later there was wild loud music from Mille's marquee and much leaping about, which the people probably thought was dancing, but it was not gracefully soundless like Mille's. When some of them grew tired or needed to be peaceful, they came into the sitting-room, where I kept them company. None of the other cats would come near all the noise and the visitors, who all thought I was the perfect hostess, which I know I am, but it made me feel purring proud all the same.

Next day, when all was quiet again, Mille danced in her marquee and the Gentle Mother came to sit at one of the tables and have some of the 'weeding' cake with Catherine, Jenny, Darling, Big Harry and Rosie, who'd spent the night in a nearby house with one of her friends. Jenny looked as white as the cake, and as if she could never run again, but everyone was quietly contented. Of course it took a few more days for the house and garden to become themselves again and Lion pretended to be grouchy about what he called 'The Disruption', but he's always loved 'You Go' so I'm not sure he meant it, and I was purr-hearted to have been part of such happiness.

Hugely pleased purrings, love Amber

2001

Dear Dear Mary,

Everything has been calmly peaceful lately, until the other day a Terrible Thing happened to Grubby who lives on the other side of the bumpy road. It goes to show how danger can come where you never expect it. His family have moving rooms of course, which have their own house with doors that go up and down with no-one near them, whereas our moving room house has a door that Jenny and Darling have to push firmly round, so we can always hear it coming. Grubby must have left it too late to go under the door as it was shutting and got squashed in it. I was keeping Big Harry company that day when Grubby's Carol came to our door holding him. It was yowling upsetting but Big Harry took them to the Clever Vet and Grubby is all right. He was bruised but not broken.

I'm sorry for Grubby anyway, because the little kitten, called Sniff, that Carol brought home has grown into a tiger and bullies both Grubby and Filth so that they can hardly call their home their own, and have to visit other houses. Sniff is much worse than Lion, who does not like Grubby coming over to our territory and they spit at each other, but I can understand why he comes. I am just glad that the little creatures Jenny brought home have grown up so nicely.

Of course Mille and Lenni are big cats now and have their own ways, as all cats do. Lenni sleeps all lolling long and languid, stretching so lengthily across the carpet or the bed that there seems far more of him than there ever could be. He is a relaxed cat and if I wash his ears, as I sometimes do, it makes him close his eyes and purr at level ten. It reminds me of when I used to wash Silvester. Mille sleeps more neatly like me, but is always watchful. She loves to curl up on Darling's chair, where he keeps his clothes at night-time, for she loves him as much as she loves Jenny.

Both Mille and Lenni are gentle, cheerful cats. Lenni is more like me for he will talk to nearly anyone, but Mille is 'family only' and doesn't like visitors. Lion's Mary loves to see us all when she comes and she and I always have a lovely purr together, but she laughs because she only sees Mille if she rushes through the kitchen, so she calls her Mille-in-a-Hurry.

If I must have other cats living with me then I can't complain about Mille and Lenni. And now I will tell you something chirrupingly funny. Neither of them are afraid of Lion, and Mille sometimes chases him! I am round-eyed incredulous that Lion, of all cats, will run away from someone I think of as a friend. As you know, Dear Mary, it is a strict rule that you never laugh *at* a cat; it is only allowed to laugh *with* a cat who is entertaining you on purpose, but I truly cannot help grinning when I see fierce Lion pounding away from soft Mille. Jenny and I smile at each other and try not to let Lion know.

Amused purrs and love,

from Amber

2002

Dear Dear Mary,

First, Happy Happy New Year, Dear Mary. I do hope you're not ill but the winter isn't an easy time, is it? As you know, I love the garden and like to spend hours and hours out there, but not when it is cold. A bitter wind is especially horrid. It gets under my fur and blows ice-breath onto my skin which makes me miserable, so I don't want to go out very much at all, do you? The best place to sit and dream and sleep is in the clothes basket on top of the warming heart and I seem to get a turn quite often, even though Lion likes it too. But he goes out more than me and as it's first-cat-in-stays-in, I do quite well. Jenny has given up putting clothes in the clothes basket, which I think is sensible. She sort of drapes them about the warming heart room and sometimes I have a shirt hanging over my head like a person, only it doesn't talk. I don't mind, it makes me more hidden and safe. Have you ever tried sleeping in a warm basket Dear Mary? It's good. I would say purr level nine.

And now Dear Mary, I want to tell you some special, wonderful news, probably purr level more-than-ten. I don't think you will ever guess what it is, however hard you try. I have another house, one that is all just mine.

When it was nearly New Year, one morning Jenny put me in a basket — not the clothes basket but the one with a top and a door that I sometimes travel in to see the Clever Vet. At first I was worried that we were on our way there, but the moving room felt different. To begin with it was the big car, not Jenny's, and there were many things in it like cheese and rubber boots. Jenny kept talking about a holiday, and though I didn't know what that was, the way she kept telling me I was going to have one made me feel it was important and I was going to like it.

Do you remember how I was always frightened of going in tin cans? I was quite surprised that I wasn't frightened this time, but Jenny was sitting beside me in the back, while Rosie was on the front seat next to Darling. I suppose he was holding the dark circle that makes the car move. Jenny certainly wasn't, as she was stroking me with her finger through the basket. Soon she opened its little door and let me come out and creep forward onto her knee, and purr some more. The big car was making a sort of rumble, a bit like a purr, and I suppose it was speeding along on the journey. I couldn't tell from Jenny's lap, but I was happy. I was sure something claw-stretchy was going to happen.

At last the big car stopped and, as soon as the door was open, I could tell from the air that we were somewhere far away from home. Jenny had put me back in the basket a few minutes before, and now she lifted me and the basket out of the car and carried me up a path and in through a door. (Actually it took her some fumbly time to get the door open because she's not very good at that sort of thing and I suppose Darling was busy with the cheese and boots and bags.) Anyway, at last she got the door open and carried me in. Of course, Jenny and Darling had to have a cup of tea (they do that a lot) while I came out of the basket and began to look around.

It was a big room with two huge comfy sofas and a good view from the long window into the garden. There were three other windows, with sills for sitting on. As well as the sofas there was a big table, which made me think of the one in the kitchen at home. It was quiet apart from the music that they like to have playing. There was nothing to frighten me and I found a sort of tunnel behind the sofa where I could lie on the soft carpet close to the great warmer on the wall. I stayed there for a long time, breathing in the new place and feeling happier and happier.

Later, I explored some more and found I was in a small house with no stairs but two good bedrooms, in which the beds were useful for going under as well as sleeping on top of with Jenny and Darling. And you see, Dear Mary, the best thing about this house is that there are **no other cats** — not one —just like when I was with you. Suddenly I had my people all to myself. I could sit with them, by them or on them, whenever I wanted. I could snuggle up to them on the bed and sleep all night close to them, purring more than level ten I should think. In the morning I felt so happy I thought I would make them laugh, so I pounced on their toes under the covers for, as I've said before, you can laugh *with* a cat but never *at* a cat.

Next morning Jenny and Darling went out, taking Rosie. They put on coats and boots while Rosie got excited because she was going too. She likes to go for walks with them but I don't much and certainly not in a strange place, and I didn't mind staying in by myself because I know that when people go out they always come back — and they did.

Sometimes they leave Rosie in the house with me, for she gets very tired as she's quite old and just sleeps on her bed on the floor — well, most of the time she does but she thinks the sofas are comfy too so, after a while, she climbs up and stretches out on one of them, which seems quite sensible to me. However, when Jenny and Darling came back the first time this happened, they both said, 'Oh Rosie', quite loudly so she could hear them (for she's going deaf) and made her get down. And the next time they left her behind, they covered the sofa with a big cloth for all her furry hairs to go on.

This house has a garden, but I didn't want to explore it, at least not without Jenny. First she just carried me out there, then put me gently on the wall so I could see if it was comfortable for sitting on and looking around. There were many birds and, over the wall, (which was a fine stone one that I shall enjoy making mine) were some animals, not as big as cows and not as black-and-white. They had a lot of shaggy fur and seemed keen on eating grass. They looked very surprised to see me but didn't appear to be fierce.

The wind was cold out there so I was glad to come indoors again, but later on that day I did a brave low run from the open window-door to the hidey safe shed, which is dark and smells of wood and black stuff in lumps, called coal. This was a good way to get to know the garden a little at a time. I would creep out and explore and then rush back to the shed. I must have done this a few times before I got cold and decided to go back indoors. Jenny told me I was brave, and I thought so too, though I have a feeling that she was watching me carefully. I believe some cats try to find their first home when taken somewhere new. Oh Dear Mary, do you remember the Unhappening! That was yowling hard for me. But I would not be so stupid as to run away from my very own new house where I am the best and only cat.

We stayed in my new home, which I have called No-Other-Cat-House, for five or maybe six nights and I watched lots of birds through the windows for they came to eat the swinging nuts and seeds. I suppose it is useful to be able to fly but I'm glad I'm not a bird; I don't like nuts and many things must be frightening when you're so small and light.

Jenny got very excited one morning about a squirrel who came to eat nuts from his own box on the tree. I thought it was clever the way he could open it up and take the nuts out, but I thought she made rather a fuss, even making Darling get up from his breakfast to look at him. Apparently he's a special squirrel because he's a different colour, not beautifully gold like me but a red-leaf colour, and he has tufty ears and a bushy tail. Anyway, I had to admire the way he could run along the stony lumpy wall and then go straight up a tall tree, running as easily as if on the ground and, as you know Dear Mary, squirrels can nearly fly.

I was very sorry when it was time to leave my No-Other-Cat-House but Jenny promised she would bring me with her each time she comes, and I'm quite surprised that I don't mind travelling in a moving room so long as Jenny's beside me. She'll never be my special person like you are Dear Mary, but she does try very hard and I do love her.

Something else good has happened too. When we got back to the big house Mille and Lenni wanted to know where I'd been and thought I was lucky. That made me feel happy and be braver. Somehow I feel I can even say 'Spit' to Lion, and actually go in the bedroom with Jenny and Darling again, and eat some of Mille and Lenni's biscuits, when I can make the huge high leap onto the window ledge where Jenny puts their food. It tastes just a bit different from mine downstairs, so makes a change now and then, and Mille and Lenni don't mind. I do not, of course, sleep on the bed in case Lion arrives suddenly to pound on Jenny, but my box in the cave is snug, and warm and dark. To have a comfortable, safe sleeping place is so important and necessary, isn't it Dear Mary?

Purring hugely, love Amber

Dear Dear Mary,

You know, in all the time since I lived with you Dear Mary, I have never believed that I would ever again be as happy as I was with you, but now that I have my own house where I'm a princess I feel much more settled. Mostly change is not good for cats but I must admit that sometimes it is purring pleasing.

Lately we have often come to No-Other-Cat-House. We spend lovely lingering times up here and I have Jenny, Darling and Rosie, and everything else, all to myself. The sheep are not surprised to see me any more and I'm quite used to their loud baas. I sit on the lumpy wall that the special squirrel runs along or I move gently in the quiet grass and listen to the silvery sounds the stream makes as it travels past No-Other-Cat-House. I watch all the many birds but don't try to catch them, for I did all that long ago and it's good just to rest and be happy.

Lenni and Mille think they came here when they were little creatures, because kittens are not dangerous. Then they grew bigger and started trying to catch the mice and birds. Apparently Mille even tried to climb like the special squirrel, who was round the other side of the huge tall tree while she scrabbled on it. She thought he may have laughed at her, which cats don't like, so she got down and washed herself, and decided she didn't want to climb the tree anyway. But now she is big she might try to chase the special squirrel, so she's not allowed to come here any more.

I am a quiet cat and don't want to chase anything (except sometimes my tail, or Jenny's toes under the covers) and that's why I can come to No-Other-Cat-House. I'm also happier at the big house than I've ever been before, now I've something which none of the others have. Lenni and Mille are friendly to me and Mille chases Lion sometimes, as I told you, which I think is funny. He's older now and, though he still tries to be bossy, I don't take so much notice. Anyway, he's not as nasty as he pretends to be; he goes all soft and windy round Rosie.

Rosie plods slowly now and doesn't go far. I may soon decide to go on a slow walk from this house too, for when we are at the big house I walk with Jenny and Rosie along the lane every morning, sometimes as far as the pond with the ducks on it. If a car or a dog comes I slide into the hedge and hide secretly until it's safe again. Jenny is trustworthy. I know she will wait for me to come out. She talks to me all the time and tells me I am brave, which is true. Sometimes Mille and Lenni walk part of the way with us, making a cat queue along the lane. We trot with our tails waving in the air. Rosie has a very low, slow wag and is usually last. Lion doesn't do walks and of all the cats it's me, Amber, who goes the furthest. This makes me happy and purring proud.

I'm considering the land over the wall of No-Other-Cat-House rather carefully as it is wide and wild, with no places to hide. However, there are no cars here except ours, and the sheep are not frightening so, when I'm ready, I may go on a wild slow walk with Rosie, Jenny and Darling. I've also been thinking a new and wonderfully hopeful thought. Now that I don't mind travelling, Jenny might one day bring me to see you where you live now. To think of that is claw-stretching.

Meanwhile, here I am Dear Mary, settled in a cosy basket, or sitting on the comfortable parts of the lumpy rock wall, or rolling on the grass under a sheltering bush in the warming sun. I think how happy I am and I purr. And this is a purr which is not just loud, more loud than level ten, but deeply long, so that it throbs through me and down, down, into the earth. It will travel tens and tens of miles to find you, to be a comfort to you, and bring me smiling to you in your heart and dreams.

With my love always,

Amber

If you've enjoyed the story of Amber you might like to read ...

A Cat in My Lap

... which tells about Jenny's early married life in rural Essex and her move to Cheshire. Her elegant prose and wry observations make this account of her life in both places a joy to read.

Jenny is not just 'a cat person' — her dogs, children, husband and many other characters play a part in the story — but it is her cats that are at the heart of the book. As different in personality as any cast of characters, some were chosen as kittens, but others came to her as strays or survivors.

Again Jo Berriman's illustrations are a delight, bringing to life all the cats who feature in the book. And, inspired by her cats, Jenny's poems further enhance the text.

This book makes the perfect gift, not just for people who love cats, but for anyone who appreciates the countryside and the gentler things in life.

Contact *Alfresco Books* on 01729 830868 to order a copy.

About the Author

Born in Sevenoaks, Kent, Jenny trained at St Andrew's and Durham Universities, then practised social work in London prior to her marriage. In 1975 she moved, with husband, sons, dog and cat, from Essex to Cheshire, where she began to write. Since then she has had several books published and been a performance poet and creative writing tutor. She has worked in many schools and also in the community with people who are disabled. Currently, she gives talks and readings, and revels in being a grandmother. She has a rescue 'demi-greyhound' and four cats.

About the Illustrator

After leaving art school in Manchester, Jo Berriman trained as a textile designer, later moving into graphic illustration in various commercial art studios, before settling on book illustration. Her first full length collaboration was with Jenny on *A Cat in My Lap* and, although semi-retired, she was delighted to be involved with *Dear Dear Mary*, where again she has sensitively captured the character of all the cats featured in the book.

Jo lives in New Mills, Derbyshire, and now paints landscapes, portraits and animals for pleasure. She has a cat called Poppy.

About *Alfresco Books*

Alfresco Books was founded in 1991 by Jen Darling, initially to publish her own walking books. Since then she has also produced books by other authors on a variety of topics — wildlife and organic gardening, travel and adventure, and others for animal lovers and children.

One of the gems of the whole collection is *Edwardian Rambles* — a magical original manuscript in full colour. Written in the early part of the 20th century it features the villages and countryside of Cheshire and the county town of Chester.

After living, working and bringing up their family in Cheshire for over 37 years, Jen and her husband relocated back to her native Yorkshire in 2004. She hopes that *Dear Dear Mary* will be as great a success as *A Cat in My Lap* has proved to be.

For a Book List call *Alfresco Books* on 01729 830868
or e-mail jen@alfrescobooks.co.uk.